THE BEST CANADIAN ESSAYS 2009

The Best

Canadian Essays

2009

Edited by Alex Boyd & Carmine Starnino

Tightrope Books

Canada Council
for the Arts

Conseil des Arts
du Canada

Tightrope Books
602 Markham Street
Toronto, ON
M6G 2L8
Canada
www.tightropebooks.com

ONTARIO ARTS COUNCIL
CONSEIL DES ARTS DE L'ONTARIO

COPY EDITOR: Shirarose Wilensky
COVER DESIGN: Karen Correia Da Silva
TYPESETTING: Jo Snyder

Produced with the support of the Canada Council for the Arts and the Ontario Arts Council.

Printed in Canada

LIBRARY AND ARCHIVES CANADA CATALOGUING IN PUBLICATION

The best Canadian essays, 2009 / editors: Carmine Starnino and Alex Boyd.

ISBN 978-1-926639-05-5

1. Canadian essays (English)—21st century. I. Starnino, Carmine II. Boyd, Alex, 1969-

PS8373.1.B48 2009   C814'.608   C2009-903915-X

Contents

Contents

INTRODUCTION

When Ezra Pound recommended that "poetry should be at least as well-written as prose" he confirmed what every journalist, book reviewer, literary critic, and magazine writer already knew: prose is hard work. It can be as economical, sensuous, and bracing as poetry, but, unlike poetry, prose has specific rules and provides specific guarantees. That's because prose is what you turn to when you want to say something about something. One really can't afford to be at a loss for words. It is an information conductor: no matter how stylish your sentences, your syntax must serve up clarity not ambiguity.

Prose is also the freelancer's medium. Written for payment, prose is a product that, in turn, is sold to consumers who inhabit a marketplace filled with distractions. The writing, therefore, needs to be lively and incisive. It needs to act swiftly on the reader. What's more, people who write prose are people who hustle after assignments. They tend to have a habit of taking on too much, which means they live a life oppressed by deadlines. There's no time, to become self-conscious or rhetorical. When such writers get in trouble, they need solutions that work on the fly. But if they're good, their instinct for expediency shares space with an appetite for artistry. They try to find new ways to build rhythm into their paragraphs. They try to find new ways to construct crisp, well-shaped sentences. The end result is a kind of belletristic grace: writing that wants us to take pleasure in the experience of reading it, but also has an overwhelming interest in making itself understood. This twofold challenge—to hold the reader's attention, while giving them news they need—is why prose plays such a vital role in building up a viable public culture.

We looked high and low for essays that displayed this kind of prose, from literary periodicals to web journals to general-interest magazines. We were spoiled for choice. "An essay," said Ian Hamilton, "can be an extended book review, a piece of reportage, a travelogue, a revamped lecture, an amplified diary-jotting, a refurbished sermon. In other words, an essay can be just about anything it wants to be, anything its author chooses to 'essay.' " Hamilton here reminds us that the term is drawn from the French verb essayer: to try on, attempt, put to the test. No surprise, then, that so many of the essays we found revel in the opportunities the form offers as a vehicle for exploration. No navel-gazing, either. Writers delivered their stories from the front lines of human experience. They addressed themselves directly, and fearlessly, to serious subjects. They worked hard to produce original approaches to important, much-covered topics suffering breezy neglect by a bored media. What this book helps prove is that, along with our talent for short stories, Canadians excel at the essay form. We have a knack for open-mindedness, feel uneasy around oversimplifications, try to square any starkly opposed positions. Growing up somewhere between American gusto and British reserve, we are perhaps well-positioned to make balanced, nuanced, valuable observations. We have a built-in appreciation of diversity and culture. We are also, by nature, generalists: we like to know many things about lots of subjects. All of which gives Canadian prose a three-dimensional credibility.

This book could have been three times as big. Selectivity, however, is not only a critical tool in the essayist's skill set (good writers learn to zero in on evocative details and relentlessly remove the non-essential) but also the main requirement of anthologists. So here are fourteen essays that, taken together, offer a topnotch primer in how to live an examined life. They are worth reading because of the skill with which they were written, but wisdom is their main selling feature. *The Best Canadian Essays 2009* is a snapshot of some of the best examples of Canadian thinking that occurred last year. Be prepared to feel as though you've come through several dozen interesting conversations.

Alex Boyd, Toronto
Carmine Starnino, Montreal

THE BEST CANADIAN ESSAYS 2009

TOO POOR TO SEND FLOWERS:

THE STATE OF CANADIAN THEATRE

Kamal Al-Solaylee
Canadian Notes & Queries

I remember the exact night I knew English-Canadian theatre was taking its last gasp. The time: November 2007. The place: the Young Centre for the Performing Arts. The production: Noel Coward's *Blithe Spirit*, a story of two dead wives coming back to haunt their easily flummoxed husband.

Dear reader: death was everywhere. Onstage, the aisles, and especially the lobby, which looked more like the setting for an organized activity at a seniors' home than the inner sanctum of a flagship theatre in the gentrified Distillery District in Toronto's east end. The competing wafts of perfumes, hair gels, and Bengay couldn't hide the stench of decay. Old people, old plays, old actors.

At forty-three, I was the youngest audience member by at least twenty years and the darkest by as many shades. Where were all the ethnicities Toronto trumpets as a mark of its world-class, cosmopolitan identity? Maybe they knew better than to show up to an event to which they were neither invited nor welcomed. Variations of the same scene (i.e., old, white audiences) have played out at nearly every mainstream theatre I've attended, from Vancouver to Montreal. My standard joke when arranging to meet someone for the first time at a performance is to say I'll be the brown-skinned guy in the lobby. It never fails.

For the moment, theatre in English Canada can still coast on the Last Great Generation—the middle-class baby boomers who show up night after night out of national pride, loyalty, curiosity, or habit. But what happens next? How can we expect Canadian theatre to survive in the coming decades when its major patrons are dying off and half of the population is disconnected from the art form as we practise it?

The answer is we can't. Nor should we be surprised. For decades now Canadian theatre has been a private party. Few of our playwrights bother to write for an audience and fewer artistic directors program with one in mind. What matters is the next grant application and whatever buzzwords jurors and corporate sponsors are looking for: "hybridity," "experimental," "multimedia," and, ironically enough, "multicultural." Ten years as a theatre critic in Canada taught me that the differences between Canadian and American theatre are not about size or money but attitude: Americans write to be heard and to talk to fellow Americans; Canadians write to impress jurors and each other. We race to win the hearts and minds of like-minded peers. Strangers can wait.

This attitude was best exemplified at the Tarragon Theatre in 2005, when it produced David Macfarlane's *Fishwrap*, a glib, barely disguised one-man show about the Toronto writer's falling stock with the editors of a certain national paper. Virtually every line in *Fishwrap* was written by Macfarlane in a direct address to his inner circle of Toronto literati and could just as easily have been contained in his annual Christmas email to them. I'm all for theatre as personal therapy but would it have killed Macfarlane or his director to share some of their me-and-my-friends insights with the audience?

As it happens, Tarragon Theatre has also produced many wonderful dramas that speak eloquently and passionately to as wide an audience as possible. I'm thinking of John Mighton's *Half Life* (2005), an exploration of memory loss and artificial intelligence, or of *Rune Arlidge* (2004), Michael Healey's wise and beautiful story of three generations of an emotionally scarred Canadian family. Both plays are motivated by a desire to share experiences—of aging, childhood innocence, and lost dreams—with an audience who can be expected to reflect on their own experiences and draw comparisons between themselves and their onstage reflections. Hidden behind these triumphs is the professional shame of being the exceptions and not the rule.

Instead of cooling their heels, impatient audiences are performing their own act—a vanishing act. Like millions around the world, Canadians now get their share of stories from television. Binge-watching *Lost*, *Mad Men*, *Heroes*, and *Dexter* has turned young and old alike into DVD junkies. How many times have you taken the train, only to be surrounded by passengers catching up on their favourite show on their laptops? The un-PC sharpness of the writing on American cable has eliminated the need to visit theatre for a dose of hard reality. The nastiest scene of Toronto playwright George F. Walker's most corrosive play looks tame beside an episode of, say, *The Wire*.

Various theatres have, of course, made valiant attempts to lure younger audiences. In April 2007, Toronto's Mirvish Productions—a company that normally trades in blockbuster musicals and light comedies—mounted *e-Dentity*, an examination of cyberspace's influence on human communication and community. Brainchild of the experimental Theatre Gargantua, *e-Dentity* started life as a very successful small production that integrated text, music, live chat, and interactive projections. But when producers transplanted the play into the cavernous commercial space of the Royal Alexandra, it bombed (subscribers were seen fleeing at intermission).

Serves them right for so cynically presuming that the old rules (build it bigger and they will come) also applied to the Web 2.0 crowd. The appeal of new media goes beyond mere visual stimulus and reaches into democratized creation and participation. That's why *e-Dentity* worked at Gargantua. The intimate stage and scale was in sync with a generation that goes online to write their own drama, star in their own production, attend the performance they want when they want. Mirvish—watching their subscribers move from retirement home to grave—were desperate for Gargantua's magic, and the hip market share that came with it. But theatre is not retail. Producers and artistic directors can't just order a new shipment of theatregoers and restock empty seats.

And what young spectator can afford Mirvish ticket prices? A smarter idea would be to follow the example of Britain's National Theatre, which, for eight years now, has been partnering with Travelex to provide tickets for ten pounds, thereby ensuring the presence of students and youth at every performance. I've been visiting that theatre since the program started, and every year I watch, jealously, as the young and multicultural audience grows. Most other major European theatres have similar plans, which are always well advertised. Whenever one of our theatres embarks on a similar initiative, the message barely gets out—and if it does, it reeks of desperation. As anyone on the mailing list of Canadian Stage Company in Toronto already knows, the special offers flood cyberspace whenever it has a box-office bomb. A current example is $25 for a limited period of twenty-five hours to see a stage adaptation of *It's a Wonderful Life*—a bargain even if the production, based on the Hollywood classic, firmly belongs in the dead theatre camp.

So where do we go from here?

Some futures aren't that hard to read. It's only a matter of time, for instance, before half the population in our major cities is either a visible minority or born outside of Canada. With such a major demographic shift literally staring us in the face, you would think that theatre professionals—who surely ride the same immigrant-rich transit system I do—would be scrambling to woo ethnic audiences (some of whom, like South Asians, come from cultures with rich traditions of public performances). If the success of the recent all-black revival of *Cat on a Hot Tin Roof* or the Hispanic-flavoured *In the Heights* is any indication, even our brothers on Broadway realize that acknowledging reality is no longer an option but the only survival strategy.

To be fair, companies with ethnic mandates do exist in Canada. Toronto's Obsidian Theatre is proudly black and Fu-Gen is playfully Asian. Since most of them can't afford their own space, they stage one or two shows a year in a subscription-basis theatre, either as part of its regular season or as a rental. This only confirms the existence of a great divide between theatre for white people (the main narrative) and another for everyone else (secondary plot). In a sense, you might say the latter camp exists on the margin of the margin. And as much as creating for the margins is a vital part of any vigorous art, the spirit of theatre is communal. It can only be felt in that exchange between performers and audiences sharing the same space, the same never-to-be-repeated moment. There is no future in segmented companies protecting and speaking to their own cliques. The self-affirming spirit of such companies needs, instead, to be part of a larger, systemic change that sweeps up mainstream theatres like the Factory, the Tarragon, the Citadel, or Manitoba Theatre Centre.

We need artistic directors and playwrights, in other words, who care about more than surviving another season, another fiscal year, another grant application. We need transformational figures who can reach all ethnicities and age brackets. We need revolutionaries who can convince the populace that theatre is *its* art form, as well as a necessary part of any healthy community, country, and economy.

On that last point, present circumstances only strengthen my pessimism. There's no way Canadians will outlast the current financial crisis without permanent damage to the fabric of our lives and some retrenching of our expenses. This may mean that when the death of English Canadian theatre is officially announced, even those who care for it will be too poor to send flowers.

THE NEW DEATH ETIQUETTE

Katherine Ashenburg
Toronto Life

Carmen Crilly was dancing with her mother to Feist's "1234" when she died. A beautiful, squirrel-cheeked baby with outrageously long eyelashes and a belly laugh that carried on and on, Carmen was born with a degenerative brain disease. At ten months, she was unresponsive and having difficulty breathing. Her parents, Catherine and Bill Crilly, gathered their older children, Ella, who was almost four, and two-year-old Mick, and began dancing in the kitchen to the kids' favourite song. "I held her head against my cheek," Catherine remembers, "and she died there in my arms as we all spun around."

Ella had made a fabric "hug" for her little sister (she traced her outstretched arms on a blanket, cut it out, and decorated it with pictures and stickers), and they wrapped Carmen in it. They added notes the family had written to her, and some toys Ella and Mick thought she would want. While the funeral home took Carmen's body away, the Crillys went up on their deck and blew bubbles in her honour.

When they reminisce about the course of Carmen's illness, Catherine likens it to a slow dripping away of her vitality, "as if someone had snipped her baby toe." At three months she had started becoming fussy and losing some of her developmental milestones, such as grasping. But her disease, called Krabbes, is so rare—Carmen had only the twenty-sixth case reported in Canada since the 1950s—that she was not officially diagnosed until she was five months old, in August 2007. The doctors told the Crillys that the average lifespan of a baby with Krabbes is thirteen months.

Carmen stayed happy and responsive until her last five or six weeks, but by nine months, she had lost her sight and needed increasing amounts of medication and oxygen. On January 12, the Crillys called their families to come and have a final visit with Carmen; it was in effect a pre-wake. After that, aside from the medical team, only her parents and Ella and Mick saw her. She ate very little at the end, and her parents didn't want people remembering her in an emaciated, uncharacteristic state. She died on January 21.

At thirty-nine, Bill is a business developer for SNC-Lavalin, an engineering and construction firm. Catherine is thirty-two and had worked as an intervener with deaf and blind children and as a Montessori teacher before becoming a full-time mother. They are used to being in control, not to having a one-size-fits-all protocol imposed on them. He was raised Catholic and she Anglican, but like many people, they have parted company with organized religion. When it came to marking Carmen's death, they could have made a perfunctory return to a religious observance—a wake, a church funeral, and burial. Or they might have opted for a radically pared-down secular service—going straight to burial or cremation, with perhaps a gathering of close family at the funeral home. But neither of those alternatives appealed to them. They wanted to commemorate Carmen's life and death, for her sake as well as theirs, with personal, custom-made rites.

The way we say goodbye to our dead is changing. Bruce Humphrey, the president of Humphrey Funeral Home, says that in the old days, when people called to announce a death, he only had to ask which church the funeral would take place in to know all he needed to make his plans. But now people are working hard to reflect the individuality of the deceased—borrowing and adapting rituals from a variety of religions or simply doing what feels right to them. Whether the service is secular or not, the possibilities for personalizing the event are multiplying: there's often a picture board, sometimes a recording of the dead person's favourite music, and even a video of his or her life. At the June memorial service for twenty-five-year-old Dylan Ellis, who was shot in front of a Richmond Street condominium, the sanctuary of Rosedale United Church was decorated with a worn pair of shoes, a well-used surfboard, and a white electric guitar plugged into an amplifier, as if in readiness for its young owner. There were framed pictures, a slide show, and sixteen speeches by friends and family.

There isn't one single cause that explains these idiosyncratic commemorations. No doubt the many deaths from AIDS in the 1980s, most of them young people who were unconnected to a church or synagogue, accelerated the popularity of personalized services. And baby boomers, who have reinvented every other stage of life, are now seeing their parents and even their peers dying. Many are deciding that one of the two most profound passages in life surely demands what Yeats called "custom and ceremony," and they have begun to put their stamp on death. In some ways liberating, the possibilities are also daunting. The ceremonies and attendant hospitality around a death can be almost as complicated as those of a wedding, which people spend many months planning. These mourners, unmoored from tradition, have a significant dilemma: at a very difficult time, they have to choreograph their own ritual, often making it up as they go along.

When they began to plan Carmen's service, the Crillys didn't want to hurry, and they didn't want someone who hadn't known their daughter presiding. They arranged for her to be cremated because they liked the idea of scattering her remains in the wind—Carmen loved wind and always laughed when a breeze ruffled her hair. Cremation would also allow them to have a service three weeks after she died, one that they could conduct themselves.

In the end they chose a church because, as Bill says, "We wanted someone to lead us into it." They craved something of a church's ambience, maybe something of its dedication to things of the spirit. On February 9, about 200 people gathered in College Street United's warm, intimate space. Many of those present had never met Carmen, and her parents' goal was to make her real to them. The parents do not remember feeling nervous or worrying about whether they would cry. "It was our duty as parents to do right by Carmen," Bill says. After a welcome from the minister, Bill read a letter to his daughter, which included a description of her "double-clutch smile." It began as "a small, impish smirk," after which Carmen would close her eyes for a second as a wave of bliss swelled up from deep inside her. When she opened her eyes, her whole being would radiate a gleaming, ear-to-ear grin. Bill talked about the life he had imagined with his daughter: bandaging scraped knees, shuddering at her first bikini, making her boyfriends uncomfortable, dancing with her at her wedding. It was not to be, but he counted himself lucky for having been able to dance with Carmen most days of her life.

Catherine read a poem she had written about holding Carmen, from her pregnancy through the baby's birth and early flourishing, through her illness and death. Now, bereft of a living baby, she encountered her daughter in the softness of flower petals, the splash of water, the laughter of Ella and Mick, the breeze that lifted her hair, and the sun that warmed her skin.

Catherine's and Bill's words alternated with three slide shows, accompanied by Jane Siberry and k.d. lang's "Calling All Angels" and two Ron Sexsmith songs, "I See Tomorrow in Her Eyes" and "God Loves Everyone" (the only place the divine surfaced in the service). In the photos, Carmen beams, sticks out her tongue, and extends her arms as if to take off. The last video, which concluded the service, consisted exclusively of footage and some sound of Carmen laughing: slowly and judiciously; helplessly at Ella, who enchanted her; then so hard that she ends in hiccups. The double-clutch smile was much in evidence. At the reception that followed, many people said the words the Crillys most wanted to hear: "I feel like I knew her."

The printed program for the service included a packet of seeds for "Carmen's Flower," a small pink perennial yarrow that blooms, as she did, in spring, summer, and fall. Only in winter, the season in which she died, is it dormant. Some of the people who left the church that day with their seeds and their CD of the songs used in the service may have thought that now that the public part of mourning was over, life would soon return to nearly normal for the Crillys. That has been the sunny modern expectation, almost always accompanied by hopes for "closure," which suggests a steel door that slams shut as soon as possible after the funeral.

Catherine and Bill don't see life after Carmen that way. For them, grieving, as Freud wrote in "Mourning and Melancholia," is the strenuous work of redefining your relationship with the dead, so that they can remain in your life. Some of the Crillys' mourning practices are distinctly contemporary: they have, for example, dedicated a star from the International Star Registry to Carmen. Others hark back to things mourners have always done, such as changing their appearance to mark their loss, or making keepsakes from the clothing of their dead. Catherine has made a quilt from some of their favourite clothes of Carmen's, and she now has a portrait of Carmen tattooed on her back. Underneath, it says, "Someday soon love," quoting one of the Ron Sexsmith songs that played at her funeral. Bill is also planning to get a tattoo, on his right shoulder.

The Crillys are blogging about Carmen on a website where parents share information about Krabbes and where many babies are commemorated. Catherine writes about the bone-weariness that grief brings. Bill writes about their bittersweet first Father's Day without Carmen, about his mixed feelings before returning to work. Recently Catherine put together a video of Carmen "dancing" for the site, including for the first time some footage of her last, unresponsive period. And on the 21st of each month, at 1:30 p.m., the time of Carmen's death, Catherine puts on "1234" and dances in her kitchen.

The movement toward a mourning that is more expressive and more personal—even more accessorized—is a swing of the pendulum away from a minimalism that has prevailed for decades. I think of it as the modernist option, and it first became prominent after World War One. Worn out by the histrionic mourning of the Victorian period and appalled by the death toll of the war, people began to reconsider death and its aftermath. Demonstrative mourning—the Victorians' black crape, elaborate funeral processions, and enforced seclusion—looked overblown and old-fashioned. As the twentieth century progressed and modern medicine leaped from triumph to triumph, it sometimes seemed as if death itself was becoming old-fashioned. Certainly it did not call for much attention.

The modernist way to cope with the regrettable and even slightly shaming fact of mortality was as minimally as possible. The wake changed its name to "the visitation" and was shortened or eliminated. The funeral became more and more understated, sometimes non-existent. Often the funeral, which included the body, gave way to the memorial service or the celebration of life, where the body is absent. Cremation was increasingly chosen over burial and a grave that might be visited. Close mourners wore bright colours at the service and returned to work very soon after the death. Now, for many people, that approach to—or more properly, that retreat from—death and mourning is no longer appealing.

The evolution of memorials like Carmen's—a secular mélange of words, music, and pictures—has been rapid. Twenty years ago, it would have been radical and strange. Philip Crawford, the vice president of Morley Bedford Funeral Home on Eglinton, says the majority of his north Toronto clientele comes from a generation that still wants a member of the clergy presiding, even though they rarely darkened a church door. (They typically say to Crawford, "We're embarrassed to ask, but can you get us a minister—one who is not too religious?"). However, their children, now in their forties, have been raised without that expectation, and Crawford believes the requests for completely secular services will multiply when they start to die.

A secular service doesn't necessarily mean one without some pomp and circumstance. At the Mount Pleasant Group of Cemeteries, mourners can release white doves, from $175 for a single bird to $450 for two dozen. The Simple Alternative funeral homes can arrange for more permanent and exotic memorials: for $2,200 to $19,000, a portion of the cremated remains can be carbonized, so you can wear your beloved as a genuine diamond. (So far, two customers have taken advantage of this option.) Also available at Simple Alternative are egg-shaped pieces of blown glass that can incorporate some cremated remains or a lock of hair, as well as papier mâché urns with wildflower seeds, so you can plant the remains and watch them flower (an innovation that takes literally the old expression "pushing up daisies"). You can also buy a papier mâché urn that floats, for an interment in water, and Thumbies, jewellery decorated with thumb- or toe-prints of the departed.

None of this would surprise the Victorians, who had a cult-like devotion to mementoes of the dead. Mourning in many cultures concerns itself with stuff—the jewellery made from hair in the nineteenth century, Catherine Crilly's tattoo and quilt, Simple Alternative's glass eggs and wildflowers—in a wish to keep something of the person we've lost. Mourning also involves gatherings of people (something else the Victorians understood) because we're missing someone. Neither fills the gap, but they can help.

Henry Furman had been married three times when he put a personal ad in the *Star* twenty-two years ago. He got sixty responses, but the first one he replied to was from Mirjam Udin. Henry was from New York, from a Jewish family. In Toronto he worked as a manufacturing consultant, moonlighting as a pianist. Mirjam, the child of an Indonesian Muslim father and a Dutch Jewish mother, had worked as a nurse, medical secretary, and translator. She had been married and divorced twice. Henry and Mirjam clicked immediately and until Mirjam's death last fall, they were soulmates as well as husband and wife.

But their happiness was clouded when Mirjam was diagnosed with breast cancer two years after they met. At that point, Mirjam asked, "Henry, what are we going to do?" He said, "Obey the doctors, and enjoy life all we can." Four times the cancer was treated, each time followed by a remission, then a return with metastasis to other organs. Henry brought Mirjam home for her final six weeks, where he cared for her in their living room, massaging her and draining the fluid that accumulated in her abdomen and lungs. He was rubbing her feet when she opened her eyes for the last time, as if she were asking permission to go. Henry couldn't say no. "Up to her last breath," he says, "I hoped it could continue."

Mirjam died at 4:30 p.m. on October 18, 2007, and he kept her body overnight. "I didn't want to give her up," he recalls. "I didn't want her to spend her last night in a funeral parlour." Although they had lived on the edge of doom for twenty years, they had never talked about a funeral or wake. All Henry knew was that Mirjam wanted to be cremated and her ashes scattered on a river she loved near Guelph.

Henry describes himself as "an official Jew" and Mirjam as both "an official Muslim and Jew," but they were only peripherally interested in those religions. "I connect to Judaism in a very weird way," he says, mainly through studying Kabbalah. But that was years ago, and now he jokingly calls himself a Judist, because he feels more at home in Buddhism. Its teachings about the impermanence of life appealed to both of them, since had lived with the threat of Mirjam's death for so long.

In addition to her Buddhism, Mirjam had reminisced about the colour, the sounds, smells, and foods of the Muslim funerals she had seen as a girl in Indonesia. Henry wanted to recreate something of that festive atmosphere to mark her death, and the result was an elaborate four-part funeral that stretched over five weeks. He mimics an imaginary conversation, with Mirjam murmuring, "Henry, you didn't have to do that," and his fond rejoinder, "Oh, fuck off, Mirjam."

At the funeral parlour the day after she died, remembering Mirjam's love of simplicity, he chose an unadorned wooden coffin with no metal. Mirjam was dressed in her everyday clothes, and Henry placed three of her favourite wooden statues on her body—an Indonesian goddess in the centre of her chest, Buddha on the left breast and the Hindu god Ganesha on the right—and kissed her goodbye.

He had trouble honouring Mirjam's only request, that her ashes be spread in Mill Creek, near where she had lived. Equipped with the ashes and a bag of multicoloured flower petals, the small group of family and friends that had assembled couldn't locate Mill Creek. Finally, they found a little river near a mill, and Henry made an executive decision: "Mirjam, this is it!" They took turns strewing her ashes in the water with the flower petals.

Three days later, there was a Buddhist funeral at a temple at Jane and Lawrence, with soft-voiced monks, the occasional gong, and prayers designed to speed Mirjam's soul to its new life. A friend played an Indonesian stringed instrument, and Henry found the service peaceful, with "no Bible thumping."

Next, he staged "a huge event"—100 people—to honour Mirjam in a more personal way. The service was held about five weeks after her death, in St. James-the-Less funeral chapel on Parliament Street. For Henry, there is nothing incongruous about his choice of an Anglican chapel: he found it beautiful and convenient to their house off the Danforth. Mirjam had been cremated there. Plus, it cost only $100 to rent, and their golden retriever, Ozzie, was able to walk around during the service.

Not that there was anything Anglican about the program. A favourite funeral poem, "Do Not Stand at My Grave and Weep," which Henry read, is mildly spiritual in the dead person's promise to be present in the wind, the glints of snow and the rain, but that was as close to religion as the service ventured. The music, Asian, Indonesian, and Western, included Henry on his keyboard accompanying a singer on "Try a Little Tenderness," a song he often sang to Mirjam. Afterward, they adjourned to the Tranzac Club in the Annex, where there was more music and a potluck feast. It was, he thinks, a pretty good simulacrum of the joyful, celebratory Indonesian funerals Mirjam had watched as a child.

About 17,000 people die in the city every year, and in 2008 half of them will be cremated. That figure is expected rise to 65 percent in the next decade. Morley Bedford Funeral Services, which caters to north Toronto WASPS, has an even higher percentage: 65 to 70 percent so far this year.

People who favour cremation see it as progressive and considerate; they tell you they don't want to take up scarce space. In fact, it's not that easy to make an environmentally responsible choice when you die. The cremation of a single body emits roughly 100 pounds of carbon dioxide during the two-hour procedure, and most mourners are against the crematorium stockpiling bodies for even a few days so as to minimize the fuel needed. Embalming, which is declining in Toronto but still common among ethnic groups that prefer an open-coffin wake, deposits loads of chemicals (formaldehyde and formalin, for starters) into the ground. The so-called green burial will probably become more common as environmental concerns escalate. It involves simple coffins of local wood, paper, or wicker, or even burial in shrouds or directly into the ground. Shallow graves are dug so that the roots of trees and other plants can benefit from the decomposing bodies, and no chemicals are used, so no plants are harmed. Canada doesn't have a natural burial cemetery yet, but several sites close to Toronto are being considered.

Thomas Lynch, North America's most respected mourning guru, has a different problem with cremation. It's become a way to "disappear" the body, to use his term. As a funeral director, poet, author, and a major inspiration behind the television series Six Feet Under, he has been an eloquent advocate of saying goodbye to our dead with rituals and symbols, as the Crillys and Henry Furman did. His ideal service goes one step further, however, and includes the body. "Everybody gets invited to the memorial service except the dead guy," he says, comparing the disembodied ceremony to a christening without the baby or a wedding without the bride and groom. Lynch stresses that the cultures that have traditionally cremated their dead, such as Hindus and Japanese, have a profound respect for the symbolism of fire, and they watch the burning, but North Americans who choose cremation have made it evasive and convenient rather than lovingly attentive. While most of us do prefer a service that is more anodyne and less raw, the presence of a coffined body at the funeral gives the occasion a visceral reality and a sadness that is entirely appropriate.

Nola Crewe's Riverdale living room is large and Victorian, with a fireplace and two wing chairs in the bay. "I'll be laid out there," Nola says matter-of-factly, nodding at the bay, "and so will my husband." It's a reasonable prediction, since in the past few years Nola has laid out her daughter and her mother in the same spot.

The wing chairs were displaced most recently for two days and nights when her 102-year-old mother died in February. Fern Crewe was embalmed at Ralph Day Funeral Home, then brought to her daughter's house to lie in her open coffin. A replica of the wedding bouquet she had carried in 1932 was placed in her hands. Friends and family came between 2 p.m. and 8 p.m. to pay their respects, drink wine, eat sandwiches, and visit. Fern Crewe's grandchildren made a playlist with songs from each of her ten decades that played continuously on an iPod during her wake. Some people, Nola admits, may have felt uncomfortable with the body and lingered in the dining room, out of sight of the coffin, but most adjusted quickly and many remarked on how civilized it was to have Nola's mother at her home.

A five-year-old great-granddaughter lifted up her baby cousin so he could see "Gran." When they touched her cold body, they decided, "she doesn't feel like Gran," and that realistic assessment also pleases Nola. A lawyer and former Toronto Board of Education chair, she is now a multi-faith chaplain at Mount Sinai Hospital and studying to become an Anglican priest. At Mount Sinai, she is shocked at how many people have never seen a dead body. "We need to bring death home, to bring it into the general conversation," she says. "We have to take the mystery out because mysteries are scary."

Although waking the dead at home strikes many as extreme, Nola can't imagine shuffling her loved ones off to a sterile, institutional funeral parlour. Why bring a body to premises that strive to look "homey," she asks, when you have a home of your own? We gather there for all important occasions, and this brings death back to the family, back for the last time into the circle of life.

When I ask Nola Crewe when her family restarted the ancient practice of home wakes, she smiles. A farm family from southwestern Ontario, they never let the custom go. When her father died some forty years ago and was laid out at home, she was twenty-one, troubled and furious that he had abandoned her. In the middle of the night, she went down to the room where he was laid out and cried, "I need you, and you up and die." She put her hands on his cold, lifeless body to shake him and realized, suddenly and with finality, that he could do nothing to help her. "It showed me the value of being alone with the dead," she remembers. "When Mother was laid out here, I came down at 3 a.m. one morning and had a nice chat with her."

Maybe Nola's ease with the dead has something to do with her faith. Certainly, what brings us solace when faced with death is a cultural matter as well as an individual one. In the old days, when your tribe or your religion told you that sitting with the dead was a good thing, many people found comfort in that, at least partly because group solidarity is welcome at a vulnerable time. Now many of us have lost those cultural underpinnings, and with them much of our certainty about mourning. Convinced that marking a death with outward observances is a natural, universal response, Nola is sure that those who don't say goodbye in that way regret it.

Mourning demands that the community gather to acknowledge the hole in its fabric, with custom and stateliness if available, with homemade expressions of love and sadness if not, and sometimes with both. It can be tempting to see that as out of date, but the demand remains. As Nola says, "We like beginnings and endings. We like some kind of ceremony. We don't like things frittering away."

GET A REAL JOB

Kris Demeanor
Unlimited

In Grade 8, I joined an extracurricular social studies club called Project Business, designed to help young people learn about supply and demand economics. I signed up because Krista Copper was in it. She had brown feathered hair, eyes like a stunned deer, and wore a corduroy jacket buttoned right up to her chin, which gave her a look of impenetrability that I found alluring. We were to make peanut brittle and sell it at lunch hour, calculating the cost of the peanuts, sugar, molasses, and labour time, and fix a price that would recoup our costs or, even better, make a profit.

The club was divided into three competing groups. I made sure I was in Krista's, and she set the strategy. The key, she said, was the quality of our peanut brittle. Her mom's was awesome, so she'd get her mom to make it. We would charge the same price as everyone else, but ours would be better, so we'd sell more. Ours was indeed better, and we did sell more. We made more money, but we used twice as many peanuts, which were the most expensive ingredient. Our expenses were nearly double those of the other groups, and we made less money than everybody else. Krista was demoted from club president to treasurer and I joined flag football.

From a slave to ulterior motives to a career in the performing arts, I've spent the past ten years cobbling together a viable existence by writing, performing, and recording original music as Kris Demeanor, often with my Crack Band. Sure, under the auspices of making a respectable living, I have made halfhearted stabs at biology, architecture, horticulture, and English literature, but none stirred in me a sustainable passion. Many people love music, and love to play it, but playing professionally requires a type of enthusiasm akin to mild but unrelenting panic. I liken it to navigating through the maze of mirrors at the Calgary Stampede as a child. It was confusing, frustrating, and everywhere was me. I would bash into the glass and cry, but suppress my sobs and get it together so Dad wouldn't have to rescue me. I'd go in again the next year.

Life as a touring musician is one of thrilling variety and profound uncertainty. I have been involved in theatre, film, public education, television, and spoken word, putting as many fingers into as many pies as I can without feeling like a cheap huckster. Most artists, in their early years, and often throughout their careers, need "real" jobs to supplement their grand ideas. By real, I mean any job with a defined payment structure, with shifts of a set time frame. When the Crack Band and I play to drunken snowboarders at the Rose and Crown in Banff for $300 and nobody listens until an insufferably insistent guy crashes the stage and plays "American Pie" to grateful screams, we call it a paid rehearsal, a punch-the-clock gig. Sometimes, a great gig pays good money; it doesn't feel like a real job when you're backstage at a folk festival chatting with Bruce Cockburn in the port-o-let lineup.

Usually, though, it's difficult to quantify where art meets making a living, or what is a satisfying experience as opposed to a perversely interesting one. Creating quality art sucks time and energy, and it takes years for the monetary payoff to come close to equaling the time and personal resources spent realizing the vision. An artist's ongoing internal debate bats around many questions: How much do I need in order to live comfortably? Will CD sales and live shows pay the bills? Should I focus on publishing and write a cookie-cutter country hit? Learn a bunch of Neil Diamond songs and do corporate parties? If I do these things, am I still an artist? Who cares? Where is the romance in being an artist of unwavering integrity when Alberta Health sends the collection agency after you? Do I party because I'm a musician or did I become a musician because I like to party?

Most musicians I know are in a perpetual state of unease, continually revisiting these questions and revising our answers, knowing that we'll be asked, at family parties, by old friends at bars, and by other artists, "So, can you survive doing just music?" We all want to look at them squarely and say, "Yes, that is all I do. I live humbly by some standards, but I stand before you, clearly surviving."

Many artists have colourful "real job" histories, though not because they have a lot of interests. They love their art, and secondary loves, such as cooking and bird watching, don't make any money. An artist's catalogue of real jobs is unique because they take whatever outside work they can, only when they absolutely have to or when it's convenient, jobs with flexible schedules, jobs devoid of deep responsibility.

By global standards, of course, we enjoy lives of ridiculous comfort and wealth (understanding this helps us through the droughts).

And, like every successful business, we're helped by the supportive "teams" we've compiled: encouraging parents and spouses, understanding bandmates, the odd fan-turned-patron, a friend with some industry clout, the Canada Council. Still, it's a tenuous existence, because not only are we trying to create decent art, we are also trying to invent our own job niches. The dangerous thing about saying goodbye to real jobs is that the more time passes without one, the more impossible it is to imagine ever getting one again. But then, the most dangerous animals are the hungriest.

Let me regress.

My first band, Alchemy—From the blackest coal, may golden melodies rise!—was desperately earnest and hardworking, a schizophrenic democracy of divergent musical styles and a level of bombast that overshot our youthful chops. Our originals emulated the variety of genres that our cover songs did: folk, folk/rock, pop/folk, rock, country/rock, reggae, punk, metal, soul, rap, folk/rap, country/metal, any style we could play clumsy homage to. We did both Dire Straits's "Sultans of Swing" and The Who's "Won't Get Fooled Again." Extended versions. Our originals had names like "These Are Your 20s" and "Ten Miles Out of Paris," all delivered with an early U2 sincerity.

We had little sense of what it meant to actually make a living playing music. We were driven by the teenaged rock star fantasy, fuelled by a burgeoning music video culture, Live Aid, and nights down at the Glenmore reservoir blasting the Springsteen live box set in my bandmate Andrew's car. Talent, ambition, and desire would be rewarded with fame, girls, and money. It's totally gonna happen, man.

For us, George Harrison was the benchmark. He was twenty-one when the Beatles really hit it big. We had until we were 21. We'd make it by then. The "it" we would make was a never defined, imaginary finish line of some kind after which we'd find all the glorious trappings of rock and roll fame and thousands of people who were as deeply affected by our music as Andrew was by Springsteen, Paul by Bob Marley, Sean by Yes, and me by Cat Stevens (shut up).

We rarely got paid for our work, highlighting the bills of several Earth Day benefits, and when we did get paid, all the money went back into the band, into gear or recording. We had the work ethic of our immigrant parents, rehearsing three or four nights a week in Andrew's basement while his parents tried to drown us out by cranking Matlock upstairs.

Alchemy would get the odd nibble, some outside encouragement to keep on playing that we would amplify in importance so the dream could be extended a little longer. Our good friend and fan, Tony, changed his last name from the difficult Ehrenreich to the authoritative Foss and became our manager. He made up business cards. A handful of groupies came to rehearsals and all of our shows. Some were girls. The local A&M rep sent our demo to the Toronto office, and the guy there said he liked my voice. He said to send more. But the strains of reality confounding expectation became too much. Our youngest member turned twenty-one. Alchemy disbanded.

In my teens, while waiting for the band to take off ("take off" being the beautifully vague signpost of success right before "making it"), I got a lot of jobs through the Hire A Student office. Landscaping, stuffing envelopes, making sandwiches at Olympic Village, officiating community soccer games: I was not discerning. I also worked for a temp agency that paid $6 an hour, doing night shifts in industrial parks.

I unloaded Hugo Boss suits from long trucks. We'd form a chain of six guys and pass the suits as quickly as possible. There was a macho air to the passing, like it was a competitive relay event, and the other temp and I were in the deepest end of the truck, starting off the chain, pouring sweat and trying to out-hustle each other. We'd take breaks in a cold white room with United Way posters on the walls, drinking pop and smoking, nobody talking.

Elsewhere, I packed pharmaceuticals into various-sized parcels for mail out. I worked next to a Québécois ex-biker turned born-again Christian named Fang (he had switched names with his German Shepherd, Étienne), who quoted scripture while we packed. He liked mentioning that there was a safe in the building containing a bag of medicinal-use cocaine worth $500,000 on the street. "There was a time I would have been tempted," he'd laugh, and he'd say it again on the next shift.

I once worked from midnight to 10 a.m. with a middle-aged guy next to a machine called the "extruder." It was a giant green steel beast. We fed it bags of small plastic pellets, and twenty minutes later it would spit out industrial-strength plastic wrap that we had to make sure got onto the spools evenly. We'd prop open the door of the plant and smoke cigarettes while keeping an eye on the machine. I'd eat the meatloaf sandwiches and drink the juice boxes my mom packed for dinner. My workmate kept repeating how insulting it was that the temp agency only paid me $6 an hour while he made four times as much. "Criminal," he'd say.

There's nothing like the knowledge you're getting totally ripped off to prompt you to seek refuge in the sleepy corridors of higher education. I spent four years at the University of Calgary getting an English degree. Those are murky times. A bar called The Den had the cheapest jugs of beer in the city. But even cheap beer adds up, so I worked at The Renoir, "Calgary's Premier Retirement Address." I wore a peach tie and cummerbund and served the residents lunch and dinner as if they were dining in a fancy restaurant every day. Perks included free gourmet food and getting invited to the rooms of the elderly occupants for war stories. "When my girlfriend and I had to move our first cadaver, we laughed!" Mrs

Swanson told me. "We laughed and laughed! We didn't know how else to handle it. It was so strange. Then, later, it wasn't strange anymore."

Going to university was an incredibly valuable experience. I learned that I should never again waste my time and energy doing something I wasn't interested in, because I'd likely do a half-assed job. Degree in hand, my best buddy Paul (friend since the crib, drummer in Alchemy) and I decided over a bottle of red that we needed to go to Europe for a year. I'd bring a guitar, he'd bring his bongos, we'd work and busk our way around. No itinerary, no plan.

Busking in Europe was the first time I made a meaningful connection between making music and making a living. When you busk, people only drop money if they like the show or if they pity you. I pity some musicians: the armless, legless, or blind; any child who looks like their parents put them up to it or is dressed in a woolen traditional costume; any opera singer who is clearly classically trained and has been abandoned by their once government-funded opera centre. But two healthy, jovial Canadian boys with beer cans and donair wrappers littered around them – I'd like to think the pity drops were the exception. People seemed to enjoy it, our fast-paced "buskerized" versions of "Country Roads" and "Chelsea Hotel." We did Spirit of the West and Barenaked Ladies, bringing Canadian music to the streets of Europe, and started injecting originals into the mix.

The money we made paid for hostel beds, beer and wine, pizza and kebabs, postage for letters home, and pirated cassette tapes of Nirvana, REM, and The Cure. It was an honest living, a source of income not based on negotiation or luck. But we also took black market labour jobs. We worked in Munich for my second cousin's landscaping gartengestaltung company, constructing fancy water gardens and streams on the properties of rich Münchener's estates. A neighbour of one client complained about the croaking sound coming from one of Dieter's water gardens. Turns out there was a district bylaw with strict regulations about homeowners' responsibility for animal noises made on their property. We pumped the water out of the pond, groped around in the mud for three hours until we found the frog, and drove it to the woods.

I worked on a mussel farm in Scotland, heading out onto the loch in a dinghy and spending my days on a floating grid of aluminum platforms attached to pontoons. We hauled up twenty-metre ropes with staggered clusters of hundreds of mussels attached and stuffed them into long sacks. After spending hours knee-deep in mussels, starfish, and seaweed, I'd be sent off with a plastic bag full of mussels. I didn't feel right rejecting the generous perk, but I had no appetite for mussels. After two weeks my caravan site was strewn with bags of mussels in varying states of stench and decay.

The need to play fast and loud to get people's attention on the streets while busking informed my songwriting style after I got back to Calgary. I came home with a handful of new songs and sketches for a half dozen more, a book of lyric fragments with notes on tempo, and a primitive, self-styled music notation to remember melody lines. There was also a confidence level I had never felt before, a strong inkling that writing and performing could be my career.

I applied for a new artist demo grant, and got it. I released my first cassette of original music, put a piece of my dad's art on the cover, and got an interview on CJSW, the U of C radio station. At the same time, I was working at the Good Earth Café, and turned down a managerial position with a salary so I could "focus on my music," a bold decision considering I had no serious income from music and no industry interest.

My brother-in-law Greg, who booked entertainment at the U of C, sat me down with a proposal: my sister Monika would sing harmony, we'd get my longtime friend Ron to play percussion, and become Tinderbox, a folk/pop trio playing all my originals and a couple of well chosen covers. In our first year together we got a gig at the Calgary Folk Festival, and over the next few years played dozens of shows in Western Canada and released a full-length CD, *No, Really, Let Go* (I was still pining for my lost love in England).

I started to learn the ropes, applying for festivals and grants, putting together a package to pitch to labels, going to industry conventions, sending recordings to radio stations, finding a good web designer and, oh yes, working on the craft of songwriting and guitar playing under various forms of soft-drug inebriation. To cover living expenses (again, all money we made went back into recording, postage, and travel costs), I worked at a health food store, stocking shelves and pilfering as much organic cheese, nuts, and meat as my conscience could handle.

By this time I was playing with my Crack Band: Diane Kooch, Chantal Vitalis, and Peter Moller. The bonds formed between musicians in the same band over nearly ten years are too deep to describe with any justice here. We share the joys and burdens, and talk about really filthy things in the car. The gigs got bigger and more varied, the money better, but it was still mostly re-invested into the music, or eaten up quickly by rent, food, and booze.

I was supplementing my income doing songwriting workshops in schools for an organization called the Calgary Arts Partners in Education

Society. I went into classes and taught songwriting with curriculum tie-ins. We'd write raps about the animal classification system ("Arthropods are invertebrates / But they still get exoskeleton aches) and compose pieces about rainforest destruction sung to Britney Spears tunes ("Oops, we killed them again / The rainforests fall / Clear cutting them all / Oh, maybe, maybe, there's something we can do/ Like stop CO_2 / The trees are innocent"). The ability to pick and choose projects and regulate their duration made the job ideal because I could tour and record without scheduling conflicts, but eventually I found myself relying on the same bag of tricks in the classes, recycling melodies, and growing impatient with the kids. I come from a long line of innovative and proud teachers.

So I quit.

My last job outside of music, or at least outside the arts, was with Paul, comrade from the seminal busking trip to Europe. I was gigging a lot at the time but had a couple of dry months ahead. Paul had his own construction business and needed a hand. I got my own tool belt and prepared myself for the classic rock that invariably gets blasted at construction sites. We painted baseboards in apartment buildings, built porches, and painted faux window frames onto stucco walls six stories up on rickety ladders. We did jobs in the newest communities on the edges of the prairie, sterile homes big enough to be orphanages, every design the same, a postage stamp lawn and three-car garage, each community adhering to a limited colour palette of earthy pastels.

The hours were flexible and it was cash under the table, but Paul and I hadn't been hanging out regularly for a few years, so each day's work would be sabotaged by a lunch-time joint, a reminiscing session, and the subsequent installing of a window upside down, or the pull of the early afternoon sun to enjoy a pint on the nearest patio. These distractions forced us to work frantically to hit deadlines. One Friday, we were trying to finish a drywalling job in McKenzie Towne before the weekend, before a sound check I had at 5:30 p.m. I was measuring and scoring sections of drywall, and in my haste sliced open my left index finger with the exacto knife. I rushed over to my guitar player Chantal's house, taught her the basic chords to half a dozen songs, and at the show did the other songs either a capella or blowing into a harmonica and stomping. That's where it ended. That was it for the real jobs.

It's been seven years since that fateful slice of the finger and I feel like an inventor who, instead of developing and marketing a really good new can opener, is trying to sell the instructions for making your own really good new can opener, with a footnote saying it's okay if you accidentally put together a potato peeler.

What I mean is that on the fringes of the working world, I can be industrious and ambitious, but in essence must create my own job description daily, and try to ascertain who it is I am delivering a service to. Some bands sell bouncy, sea-of-no-cares escapism. Some sell free-floating adolescent aggression. Some are the soundtrack to fashion. Some have a target demographic that must be keen on word-heavy, satirical story songs about immigrants, the suburbs, dead elephants, police murder, and gambling, each in a markedly different musical style.

The questions get more existential. Have I turned my back not only on real jobs, but also on the real world? Will my songs become intellectual exercises, using the lives of others as fodder like a tick feeding on a plump host? Will vitality and experimentation be silenced in a bubble of self-indulgence and complacency? Should I dumb it down for the masses? Are the masses wrong? Who are the masses? Who knows a cheap accountant?

Ultimately, all I need to know I learned from Krista Copper. I will do whatever is in my power to make the best peanut brittle I can, for as many people as I can, for as long as I can, and in case of a shortfall, hopefully Krista's mom will help pay for the next batch of ingredients. Regardless, I won't quit to play flag football. This is a full-tackle game.

WHERE THE MUSKOX ROAM

Jessa Gamble
Up Here

"Try not to want it so much," says John, as I scour the barrens with binoculars. "You've gotta think like this: If the muskox want to see me, I may be available, I may not." Make them come to me? It's easy for him to say—John Squires and a fellow Colorado engineer booked this trip on a whim a few weeks ago, whereas I've been waiting for years. But I give it a try. "Have your people call my people," I offer unconvincingly to the scrubland around me. The mosquitoes sense the carbon dioxide in my breath and buzz more frantically, but there's no stampeding of muskox hoofs. I put down the binoculars, defeated. I've never learned how to use them properly anyway.

I've heard the Thelon Wildlife Sanctuary described as the Circumpolar Serengeti, a fragile yet subtly rich ecosystem. Standing on an esker in this giant triangle of tundra on the central Barrenlands, I'm not convinced. It seems like nobody's home, and I could forgive an exploration crew for thinking this place was made for mining and otherwise valueless. Lonely and melancholic, this place could pass for a dead planet tagged by an intergalactic fleet for resource extraction.

Maybe it's just my despair talking. It's day eleven of a fourteen-day canoe trip down the Thelon River, and nothing has come easily. At the very beginning of the trip we were stranded in the Dene village of Lutselk'e for four days, finally having to fly back to Yellowknife and onward to the Barrens, doubling our costs. We've been paddling nine-hour days like galley slaves trying to make up for lost time, and the bugs are unbelievably brutal. If I get to see a muskox again, it'll all be worth it, but we're already past the "Welcome to Nunavut" sign on the riverbank, signifying the border between the Northwest Territories, through which most of the river flows, and Nunavut, in which it terminates. So far, we've seen no trace of them. My best and last hope is the hike that lies ahead: the journey to Muskox Hill.

My first encounter with a herd of muskoxen was terrifying and bewitching, and I've been in love with the things ever since. A few years ago on the Northwest Territories' Horton River, not far from where it meets Franklin Bay on the Arctic Ocean, our Inuvialuit guide Enoch spotted the elusive beasts on a high tundra plain, and we scrambled up the hillside to get a closer look. It was the smell that hit me first—a potent barnyard whiff of manure. Then the adults assumed their defensive circle around the calves in response to our arrival. Although I

25

was almost charged by a bull later that day, the sight of a herd of Ice Age bovines stampeding across the tundra left me craving more.

Stumpy-legged with a lumbering, rocking-horse gait, the muskox was once thought by certain Inuit groups to be the spiritual counterpart of the bowhead whale. The long, dark coat, curving horns, and a foul reek add menace to the cetacean impression, but when a herd decides to run, its flight is imbued with grace and agility (think of the elephant ballerinas in Disney's original *Fantasia*). Flowing hair blends with the waving summer grasses of the tundra. I try to imagine them fending off scimitar cats and steppe lions in the Pleistocene era. A wooly mammoth would not be out of place on this landscape.

In 1927 the Thelon Game Sanctuary, through which my group is canoeing, was created with the mandate to guard around 250 remnant muskox from the over-hunting that had devastated them. Globally, their numbers were as low as 13,000. Protection worked. Thelon muskox populations have increased ten-fold, and the worldwide figure could now be as high as 170,000.

Sailing the Thelon via canoe, David Livingstone, the director of renewable resources and conservation at Indian and Northern Affairs Canada, sees the muskox of the Thelon as an exception within an exception. When I'd met him in a Yellowknife coffee shop a month before my trip he was the only guy in shorts and a T-shirt, stubbornly observing the nominal summer. "It's not just about saving the muskox anymore," he said, but about protecting the whole Thelon eco-system— an oasis of moose, caribou, and, in protected pockets, glades of spruce trees well above the normal treeline.

Political attention has been channelled increasingly toward the Thelon ever since the formation of Nunavut split the refuge in two, explained David Livingstone. Although it's a protected area on both sides of the border, only Nunavut's side has a management plan. In the NWT, the Akaitcho First Nation and the Métis have interests in the Thelon, and they've have opted not to sign onto any plan until their respective land claims are settled. Nunavut went ahead with their plan even though, arguably, they have the strongest immediate incentives to exploit the area economically. Livingstone was instrumental in drafting the plan but thinks it unnecessary: "What's all the fuss about?" he asks, rhetorically, "Just leave it alone. And leave the boundaries alone. There's talk of expanding it, but once you open that can of worms, you could lose more than you gain."

With uranium at its dearest in three decades, there's a real possibility that reopening the border debate could be disastrous from a conservation standpoint. Plans are underway to mine the element from sandstone formations just beyond the refuge boundaries, and even that could have downstream effects. Then again, the immediate concerns could be rendered moot by global warming. Climate change is expected to spread the boreal forest north, and winters up here are milder already. There are even reports from Inuit hunters of muskox huddling on the ground during freak wintertime sleet-storms, only to become literally frozen in place, their long guard hairs welded to the ground.

John Squires is mostly amused by my fixation with finding muskox. With a square jaw and smile lines, he has "successful American CEO" all but written on his forehead. An early riser, Squires would greet my morning emergence from my tent with a cup of coffee and a casual: "You just missed the muskox."

Packed with him was a device that turned into an unlikely keystone of the trip: A portable version of Wikipedia—the web-based encyclopedia fast becoming a compendium of everything known to humankind. We'd use the thing to determine how to fend off bugs, settle bets about history, and read entries to the group like campfire stories. On the day before our trip to Muskox Hill, Squires asked the oracle about the Thelon Wildlife Sanctuary and took the wind right out of my sails. "There are just over 2,000 muskox in the 142,400 square-kilometre area of the Thelon drainage basin," he read. Given that the beasts would be clumped in herds, that pegged our chances at slim. We only had a 200-metere strip of visible tundra on either side of the river before the first high ridge obscured our view. If the beasts weren't on the banks, they might as well be on the moon.

Early in the day we were to reach Muskox Hill we ran into Lee Sessions, who suggested we might indeed find muskox there. Hailing from Portland, Oregon, and a veteran of Arctic river-tripping, Sessions was waiting for his pickup plane at a narrowing of the waters known as The Gap. He fished out old maps from his previous trips, marked up with notations like "Campsite, Day #3: Bear" and "Fox's Den." "It's not easy walking, but it's worth the trip to Muskox Hill," he assured us, pointing at a target of concentric circles on the top of the map. "I've seen muskox standing right on the hill itself."

After another few hours paddling, we spot the prominence—four kilometers north of the riverbank, but visible from much farther away due to its pancake-flat surroundings. It's the only pingo, a mound of earth-covered ice, known to occur within the Thelon Wildlife Sanctuary, and it's probably the farthest south of any in the Canadian Arctic. From my perch on the first ridge out from the river, I see it's a mature one, slumped in the middle from exposure and the melting of its ice core. It looks like a sparsely vegetated volcano.

Between me and Muskox Hill there's nothing but brambly waist-level brush, locked together by thickly-entwined branches. Looking more closely at the terrain I must cover, I see octagonal patterns on the ground. Before I'm told this is a common tundra formation (formed by freezing and thawing), I imagine these are some of the prehistoric tent rings advertised as archeological features of the area. Pre-Dorset hunters used sites like Muskox Hill to sit for hours waiting to spot game. Take down a muskox, and they would have scapulae for skin stretchers, a cranium for a chamber pot, skin for mittens and a boatload of meat.

Then guns and trappers and traders came and dealt muskox a sucker-punch. In the late 1800s, the animals were hunted beyond any sporting chance of replenishing themselves. If it wasn't explorers looking for the Northwest Passage or adventurers seeking the last remains of the Franklin expedition, it was Nordic whalers or Hudson's Bay Company traders buying hides of *le boeuf musqué* from aboriginal communities. More importantly, they didn't leave enough for me.

Our group hacks its way through the bushes, sealing bug shirts, and sweating buckets. Our arms and backs are strong from hours of paddling, but our legs have forgotten the feel of hard use. The ivory pingo gets larger every time I look up. I don't see any telling black dots (potential muskox), but I'm looking forward to the climb itself, and the view from the top. The willows keep getting taller, and I'm panting by the time I reach the last row of them. In the final few metres between me and what looks like open space around Muskox Hill, the bushes tower above my head, and the ground turns swampy. Never mind, the water filling my shoes will cool me off a little—as long as the bog doesn't suck me down. One more branch clawing across my face and I'm out.

Oh.

The space between the willows and the hill is, I see to my dismay, a moat. It must be a seasonal one, but it's huge and impassable. I gaze up wistfully at the pingo, resigning myself to saving the climb—and the muskox—for another year. Still, as I take a few swigs of water and look around I have an urge to walk into the moat, slosh past the pingo, step up onto the opposite shore and walk out onto the Barrenlands. My group could watch me run away for weeks, as the saying goes. I wonder if the impulse has something to do with the tendency for things to move from high concentrations—such as lonely huddles of paddlers grouped around a pingo—to low, the largest wilderness area in North America, allegedly sprinkled with muskox. I suppress my urge to seek out the beasts and turn back toward my canoe.

LOST IN TRANSLATION

Nicholas Hune-Brown
Toronto Life

On the evening of April 12, 2008, Wilson Chan, the managing editor of *Sing Tao Daily*, and his editorial team gathered in their stark, fluorescent-lit office at Adelaide and Parliament to put together the next day's newspaper. Reporters worked in one area, translators in another. On the building's ground floor, an enormous printing press spat out the reams of local reporting, Hong Kong pop culture and news from China that make *Sing Tao* the number one Chinese newspaper in Toronto.

Since 1998, when Torstar purchased a majority share in the paper, *Sing Tao* editors have been allowed to translate and reprint their choice of *Star* stories—a significant advantage for a thirteen-person news department engaged in fierce competition with three other Chinese dailies. That evening, the editors selected a piece by *Star* reporter Nicholas Keung about Chinese Canadians' response to recent protests in Tibet, a topic that was dominating the news. Headlined "Chinese Canadians conflicted on Tibet," the story painted a nuanced picture of the local reaction to the Olympic torch protests. According to Keung, Chinese Torontonians were proud of their homeland and angry at the West's attacks on China, but they were also critical of the Chinese government and its human rights record. The article quoted Gloria Fung, a Chinese Canadian political observer, and Cindy Gu, publisher of a free anti-Communist government newspaper called *The Epoch Times*, both of whom accused the Chinese government of trying to equate patriotism with party loyalty, of using nationalism as a tool to stay in power.

When *Sing Tao* arrived on the streets the next morning, Keung's article ran on the front page. The byline said "Special from the Toronto Star," but Keung's article and the *Sing Tao* translation were two very different pieces. In *Sing Tao's* version, Gu's and Fung's comments had been removed, as had a section that described Taiwan's resistance to the mainland. Some of the quotes had been altered to mirror the Chinese government's official line on the protests. In one, the word "Tibetans" had been replaced with "Tibetan separatists"; in another, the words "so-called" were placed in front of "human rights abuses." The translated story began with two new paragraphs accusing the West of one-sided reporting and offering this summary of the situation: "Most immigrants from mainland China stand on the side of the Chinese government and support the suppression of the rampant Tibet independent forces before the Beijing Summer Olympics." The headline had been changed as well:

"West uses Tibet issue to attack China, inspiring patriotism among overseas Chinese."

The article set off a ripple of protest among Chinese media watchers. Ten Chinese Canadians sent a joint letter to the *Star* expressing concern over *Sing Tao's* translation, which they said had introduced a "propagandist and demagogic slant into the reportage." An article in the April 17 issue of *The Epoch Times* accused *Sing Tao* of parroting the Communist line on Tibet. Torstar executives tried to distance themselves from the translation. When *Sing Tao's* president and two editors from the Star met with the letter writers, they explained that Torstar wasn't responsible for its sister publication's editorial decisions.

From the Star's perspective, the Keung translation was an unfortunate blip in an otherwise smooth and profitable relationship. In many ways, the Torstar–*Sing Tao* partnership is a model for twenty-first-century publishing in Toronto, a blueprint for other newspapers looking to break into the immigrant media market. Mainstream newspaper circulation is declining, but the ethnic press is booming, doubling its combined circulation in the past five years.

In April, Sun Media got into the game, announcing it had signed an agreement allowing it to buy 50 percent of the three-year-old *Today Daily News*, a *Sing Tao* competitor. But while the benefits of these partnerships are obvious—increased advertising dollars, better brand recognition and access to a growing group of future English-language newspaper readers—there is a cost, and it's readers who end up paying the price.

Since the first small papers began appearing in Toronto grocery stores and restaurants a century ago, the Chinese press has been a vital part of Chinese Canadian life. From the expatriates of my grandmother's generation to the mainlanders setting up homes at the edges of the GTA today, Chinese Canadians have long depended on the local press to provide an instant community, a voice for their interests, and a kind of bridge between worlds—a connection to the motherland as well as an entryway into their adopted home.

The Chinese press has always reflected the political upheaval happening overseas. In the 1910s, the Guomindang, China's Nationalist Party, began setting up papers across Canada with the dual goals of creating sympathetic readers and raising funds. In the '20s, Guomindang-backed papers clashed with political rivals in newspaper wars that spilled off the page and into the streets, leading to legal battles, violence, and even the assassination of a Vancouver editor.

The modern era of the Chinese newspaper war has been much less bloody and far more profitable. It began in 1978, when Hong Kong newspaper magnate Sally Aw started publishing a Toronto version of *Sing Tao*. Aw is the kind of newspaper tycoon that inspires made-for-TV movies—an Asian Conrad Black. In 1954, she inherited two Hong Kong papers from her adoptive father, Aw Boon Haw—the flamboyant entrepreneur who made his fortune selling Tiger Balm—and single-handedly expanded them into a global empire with a reach that executives liked to brag was second only to the *International Herald Tribune's*.

When *Sing Tao* began printing in Toronto, there were less than 300,000 Chinese people spread across Canada. (Today there are 1.2 million.) Competition came in 1993, when Ming Pao, another respected publication based in Hong Kong, opened a Toronto office. Ming Pao put out a quality product with full-colour pictures and heaps of Hong Kong news, sparking a newspaper war—poaching talent, cutting cover prices, adding free magazine inserts—that continues to this day.

In the run-up to Hong Kong's reunification in 1997, the Chinese government began quietly courting the region's newspaper owners to ensure the press was sympathetic to China. It was a variation on the premise that supports much of modern China's success: when your carrot is access to a market of a billion people, you usually don't even need the stick. Though *Sing Tao* was traditionally aligned with Taiwan and often critical of Chinese Communist Party policies, Sally Aw was wooed intensely. Her father was an anti-Communist who had sided against the CCP in the Chinese civil war, but his reputation was posthumously rehabilitated and he was declared a patriot. Aw family land that had been confiscated was returned, and in 1992, in a scene few could have imagined just a few years earlier, the *Sing Tao* owner was greeted in Beijing by the Chinese President Jiang Zemin. Shortly afterward, Sing Tao's coverage lurched jarringly toward a pro-government position. In 1998, the government decided not to prosecute Aw in a circulation fraud case because, according to the Secretary for Justice, it was not "in the public interest."

That same year, Aw sold the majority of her Canadian holdings to the *Toronto Star* for $20 million, and in 1999, facing bankruptcy after a series of poor business moves, she sold the rest of *Sing Tao* Holdings. Today the parent company is owned by Charles Ho, a tobacco magnate and a member of the Standing Committee of the Chinese People's Political Consultative Conference, a position held by only the most loyal Communist Party members.

Like most editors in Toronto's Chinese newspaper industry, Wilson Chan has spent time at a number of publications, skipping between *Sing Tao*, *Ming Pao*, and *Today Daily*, before rejoining *Sing Tao* a year ago. A middle-aged man with a small frame and an ingratiating, even sheepish smile, Chan seems a little worn out from his thirty years in the business. When we met in his office, a sparsely decorated room with stacks of old newspapers by the door, Chan had just finished his "global meeting"—the daily conference call between *Sing Tao* editors around the world in which they discuss the news of the day and decide what to run on tomorrow's front page.

When I ask Chan how his paper covers sensitive subjects like Tibet, he tells me that *Sing Tao* is objective. "We are impartial. We just print the story if there is a story. We try to balance. This is basic journalism."

In fact, the Chinese papers seem to be intentionally scrubbed of the traditional forums for comment or opinion: they don't print local editorials, rarely publish commentary, and, though they're frequently courted by Canadian politicians, never make political endorsements. The days of openly ideological newspapers battling it out in the editorial pages are long gone. Editors from *Sing Tao*, *Ming Pao*, and *Today Daily* agree that, despite differences in packaging, each shares a similar apolitical attitude. "I think as far as the editorial policy is concerned, I don't see much difference between us and our competitors," Chan says.

In 2001, *Sing Tao* began reprinting articles from Xinhua, the official press agency of the Communist government, or what Reporters Without Borders calls "the world's biggest propaganda agency." According to Michel Juneau-Katsuya, who was Chief of Asia Pacific at the Centre for International and Strategic Studies from 1995 to 2000, the Chinese government attempts to influence Chinese Canadian newspapers by putting pressure on vulnerable writers and editors. "The editors will regularly have visits from the consular office or the embassy or will have to go back to China for one reason or another. It is 'guided.' The pressure is extremely important. If you don't write what you're supposed to, you're out of there."

One veteran Chinese Canadian editor tells me writers are in a difficult situation. "Most editors and reporters are afraid to criticize China," he says, and explains that occasionally journalists are pressured by the Chinese consulate, usually indirectly, through local community members who give journalists pointed "advice" about their work.

The Chinese government's influence on local papers is not lost on readers. Tam Goosen, an immigrant, school trustee and active community member, has been reading the newspapers for years. She says she's seen them lose their objectivity over the past decade, but thought a partnership with a mainstream paper would help. "When I saw that the *Star* had purchased *Sing Tao*, I had high hopes. The *Star* is a progressive newspaper, so I thought they would have a good influence." Since then, though, she says she's watched the paper lose its voice, translate more and more *Star* articles, and become less and less objective. "As someone who's been in Toronto for a long time, I really feel sad," Goosen says. "The *Star* should be concerned. This is supposed to be their paper."

If anyone at Torstar should feel ownership of *Sing Tao*, it's the vice president of business ventures, Carol Peddie. She's been there since day one, when her predecessor and mentor, Andrew Go, advised the *Star* to buy a stake in the paper. Go, the son of a former *Sing Tao* publisher in the Philippines and a family friend of Sally Aw, had a deep understanding of the business. When he shepherded the deal in 1998, Peddie did the due diligence, and when Go retired four years later, she took the reins as CEO.

As the daughter of English immigrants, Peddie says she understands how important a newspaper can be to new Canadians. She speaks enthusiastically about cracking a complex market with shifting immigration patterns—mainland versus Hong Kong Chinese, Cantonese speakers versus Mandarin speakers. "Once you start drilling down into these different segments, it really is an interesting marketing opportunity," she says. And a profitable one, too. In 2007, advertising profits for Torstar's jointly owned Metro newspapers and *Sing Tao* grew by 22 percent, while the flagship *Toronto Star's* profits fell by 3.9 percent.

When I ask her about *Sing Tao Hong Kong's* pro-China position, Peddie seems genuinely surprised. "To my knowledge, I have not seen *Sing Tao* taking a pro-China stand." She says the CSIS statements about Chinese government influence are ludicrous. "Never once since I've been associated with this company has anyone from Hong Kong ever said to me, 'You've gotta do this,' or 'I want you to do this,' or 'I want you to take this position.' Absolutely not. There's no way Torstar would be associated with it if that were the case." Peddie admits, though, that the fact that she can't read Chinese makes it difficult for her to monitor exactly what's happening in the pages of *Sing Tao*. She also says that, as far as she knows, no one at Torstar actually reads the paper.

About the Nicholas Keung debacle, Peddie says the translation was regrettable but simply the result of one individual's careless work. "People make mistakes, that's all there is to it." She encourages critics to look at the rest of *Sing Tao's* coverage of Tibet, which she describes as "very, very fair and very, very balanced."

She's wrong. The translation of the Keung article is far from an isolated incident. Throughout March and April, *Sing Tao* published a number of translated pieces from which facts and comments critical of China had been removed. In their translation of a Canadian Press article from March 20, *Sing Tao* editors removed numerous paragraphs that detailed the death toll in Tibet, the "harsh response" from Chinese authorities, and comments from Ontario Senator Consiglio di Nino, who said, "The fear is that hundreds, if not thousands, of Tibetans are being rounded up beyond the prying eyes of the world and may face lengthy imprisonment and torture as acts of retribution."

Half a million Chinese Canadians live in the GTA. They come from different backgrounds, with diverse experiences, languages, and ideas. But even as the community has grown more varied and complex, Chinese Canadian newspapers have become more narrowly pro-China, with none of the dissent, debate, and political freedoms you'd expect from publications owned by Canadian media companies.

The latest partnership, between Sun Media and the upstart *Today Daily*, seems headed down a similar path. *Today Daily*, which promised to take on its deep-pocketed competitors by concentrating on local news in a way that would appeal to immigrants from mainland China, will now translate stories pulled from Sun Media papers across Canada. Its publisher, Herbert Moon, began his career as an accountant for *Sing Tao* in 1978. Moon claims his paper is entirely Canadian owned—which should, in theory, free it from the political pressures and obligations felt by its rivals—but, in fact, *Today Daily's* shareholders are a closely guarded secret (though Moon admits that Sally Aw contributed to the start-up costs). And like its rivals, the paper relies heavily on news from overseas.

Moon tells me his editors pull articles from a variety of sources and that each piece is carefully labelled. But in a recent issue, twenty-four stories in the paper's mainland China section had been picked up from the Beijing-controlled newspaper *Wen Wei Po*, which has essentially acted as the voice of the Communist government in Hong Kong and Macau for years. After the Tiananmen Square massacre in June 1989, twenty *Wen Wei Po* journalists quit en masse, reportedly claiming the government was trying to "brainwash" them into reporting that only twenty-three people had been killed.

Toronto Sun publisher Kin-Man Lee seems unconcerned about *Today Daily's* ownership or editorial content. He positions the partnership as strictly business and sees no reason to complicate things. Lee offers a blunt summation of the way mainstream papers view their partners. "What we do know is that the demographics are Chinese, and that is one of the target demos that we're looking for at the *Sun*."

HELEN KOENTGES

Chris Koentges
Swerve

There will be more blooms this spring—the cactus grew at least ten feet last year. They will open around nine in the evening and then close at the first gray light of dawn. I'll sit out there with a glass of red wine and the lights out.

When I tell people about the blooms, about how they open around nine and close before sunrise and only do this for one night of the year, they always ask, "Is that all?"

Yes. That's all.

—Charles Bowden, "The Bone Garden of Desire"

The key term in Glioblastoma Multiforme (GBM) is multiforme. (Please bear with me through the science of this.) Multiforme means that there are multiple forms of cancerous cells, glioblastoma means that these forms are exceedingly malignant. Consequently, GBM always evolves toward:

      (a) its most malignant form—which is also:

      (b) the form that makes it most difficult to destroy.

And so you already see the paradox: by treating GBM—if you choose to treat it—you are, by definition, creating a stronger, more resistant mutation with each attempt. Craniotomies. Radiation. Temodol beyond the bounds of the clinic's established protocol. Experimental virus therapy. Green tea, fresh dandelion, a poisonous cocktail of intravenous Carboplatin mixed with the maximum dose of Tamoxifen—the shock-and-awe that almost wipes GBM out one day only creates an increasingly awesome mutation of it the next. On and on until you're left with something indestructible growing inside your brain, until one day there is no more space left inside your brain for it to grow.

The alternative? Well, researchers have witnessed the mass of an untreated GBM tumour double in a week, then double again, and again, and again until—well, GBM seldom fails. And that's something to be said on GBM's behalf—it is efficient. We are a culture that respects efficiency above all else. Such is the calibre of GBM's efficiency, in fact, that it is scientifically quantified by the prognosis: "six months (give or take)."

Cancer can receive no higher compliment than "six months, give or take." And that will be the last it gets from us here.

I would see my good friend every second week. That's what we'd try for, at least. He lived down the street from me in Kensington and we'd meet at a pub down another street, called the Kensington Pub. There were fake Irish places and lounges with fancy names up and down other streets, but back then my friend and I liked things to be as straightforward as possible.

So we did not believe in small talk. We'd shake hands, assume our usual stools along the bar, take a deep breath, and set to drinking ourselves near blind. This was our routine. It was straightforward. It filled me with immense joy. If I could be anywhere in the world right now, it would be on my way to the Kensington Pub to meet my friend for a beer.

What I found most comforting about those evenings was the way my friend always asked, "How's your mom?" when I'd arrive.

I'd tell him how things were changing, how it was becoming less possible to pretend they weren't. We'd shake our heads earnestly, like old men. Then I'd ask, "How is she?" and he'd tell me how his fiancée, in her mid-twenties, was steadily kicking the crap out of ovarian cancer. We'd nod our heads in understanding. That this was how such things had to work. Our updates never took more than a minute—they weren't token, mind you, because everything was communicated in that minute. We'd wait quietly for the head on the Guinness to settle properly, then launch into Stampeders football and American literature and India. All that is worth talking about in life.

In the last year of those conversations, I realized that, except for the American author Richard Ford, neither of us believed in anyone who even remotely approached a "hero." And that was the one sad part about our routine. Because my friend and I once based our lives around heroes. Without them, it seemed kind of pointless.

I've read a hundred times—I've been told at least a hundred times—that a life does not come down to, of all things, one's "battle with cancer." You know what? It doesn't and it does.

The prognosis for GBM is, as I said, six months, give or take. She lasted for thirty-six, and if you'd been around for those thirty-six, you'd know what I mean when I say "everybody's different." And you'll also know what I mean when I say I don't mean that in the way you think I do.

If you don't know what any of that means, don't worry. Because this is what you should know; this is what she taught me in those thirty-six months. It's what I'd like you to learn because I know you're facing your own indestructible acronyms, and every little trick helps.

It works this way: GBM seldom fails. The key term being seldom. Because . . . there are times. We threw everything but the kitchen sink at

GBM, and at that moment when we tried to rip the sink from the wall, it hit me that she had been on another track all along.

Over those last thirty-six months, her fridge was a jungle of cooking jammed inside different shapes of Tupperware. Not cooking like at restaurants. I mean *cooking*. Packed plastic and glass and space-age containers, which became immensely engrossing to me because I am voyeuristic, and these were windows into the way other people lived. People with means and people with less, sloppy people and neat people, busy people and people with time. People emptied their gardens into these containers, they transferred the insides of humongous tins from Costco, they poured in all they knew how to do, and then they mixed in fresh garlic. Pea soup, cabbage rolls, quinoa salad with pine nuts, mulligatawny soup, pain au chocolat (delivered one morning by express post from Montreal), Stilton cheesecake, cheese biscuits from the Georgia that isn't the Georgia where Atlanta is but the Georgia where people live to be 125, grape Jell-o, borscht, giant bricks of banana bread, ice-cream pails jammed with curry, fancy Pyrex packed with frozen macaroni lasagna, four variations of spaghetti sauce, five-alarm chili (which I once mistook for the fourth spaghetti sauce), half-a-dozen kinds of casserole, a twenty-pound turkey cooked and stuffed—and too much chocolate to count (because like the magnet on the front of her fridge said: "The only thing better than a friend is a friend with chocolate").

The fridge, even though it was never big enough, became the equalizing force of so many private lives. At any given moment it held every known manner of food in existence, all bound by a single trait: grace. It dripped and drizzled with grace. It was basted in grace. And so there wasn't one bite of one dish that didn't make my tongue tingle. I've eaten in restaurants around the world, and pilfering from her fridge was the first time I knew that a tongue could tingle. So I like the term cooking better than cuisine. And I think that has to do with the cook.

The famous paradox of being human is that we are both living and dying at the same time; every day that we live, we are implicitly one day nearer to our eventual death. The paradox of treating GBM is that by trying to kill it, you implicitly turn it into new, mightier, and more diffuse forms of itself until these forms are such that they cannot be destroyed with any treatment but the inevitable final one.

It is these two paradoxes that she so shamelessly hijacked. Because it seemed to her that if GBM were going to mutate into another form— many other forms—then she would let her own irrepressible qualities run wild into even more forms than that. If it came down to her forms and unfaltering four-dimensional systems of distribution versus GMB's, well, then she knew she'd have the sucker licked. That was the first trick, but now I'm suddenly nostalgic for how she tackled the second. Because the great marvel of watching her die—when it became defined to her as "dying" instead of "living"—was that I don't think I ever saw such a consistent and fervent exhibition of life. By that, I mean she savoured every single moment of living in spite of a future that did not exist. I know that's difficult to grasp, I'll sum it up with three noteworthy things I saw, because in these lie the mythology of what she has become.

The first:

When the fridge at her house was filled with more cooking than it could hold, I tried to sleep in a chair on the sixth or eighth or tenth floor of the Foothills hospital (they always put her on even-numbered floors). It's 3:45 in the morning—I note the time carefully. The hospital is draped in snow. The floor—let's call it the eighth—is asleep, and all of a sudden she shoots up from bed.

All week she's been given a bunch of miscellaneous neurological scores, such as the "Karnofsky" score. Not to mention the MRI score, and if you don't trust a picture of the inside of the brain, then there are the seizures that shake her body violently, or the fact that she can neither walk nor talk anymore. She's been shifted to the charge of the neurologist, who hasn't yet learned what the neuro-oncologist had learned; so that the morning brings a team, as they have come the morning before and the morning before that—a bleary-eyed team of residents and nurses—discussing her case in a way that indicates she is not in the room. When they do happen to address her (because, actually, she is in the room), it is in terms of "all the tests you have flunked, miss"; their method of address is how one might address a plant that is dying.

And so, 3:45. The eighth floor. She shoots up from bed with this . . . this pissed-off look on her face. And I'm amused. Because I've never seen anyone who has never looked even mildly pissed about anything in her life look as suddenly peeved as this mild-mannered middle-aged librarian now looks.

"Wanna go for a walk?" I ask, the third or fourth or fifth night in that chair.

And dammit.

It takes her all of six seconds to groan and move her legs, which have stopped working, over the left edge of the bed. She drops them into a pair of colourful sandals on the floor. She uses my arm to pull herself up (after glaring impatiently as I untwist out of the chair). She loses her balance for a half second as the room spins—like even the stupid walls want her to get back down in bed. She turns her glare from me to the stupid walls, and then breaks into a smile, which is the smile of primetime Nike commercials, and she starts walking. We get to the door, and I flash a look like, "Not bad, but maybe you should go back to the bed and get some—

But she's already out the door.

Then halfway down the hall.

And I, who has supposedly learned long ago not to be surprised by anything she does, am straining to catch up.

So, okay, that looks like your room, I point when we've completed a lap of the floor.

The grin creeps farther up her cheeks, cracking the cleft of drool that has dried there over the night. You see, now she's making me feel like a dork. Because she doesn't even acknowledge that there is a room, that she has any tie to this place whatsoever. She barrels past it. Then past it again ten minutes later. Then twelve minutes later. Then fifteen minutes later. Lap after lap after lap. Until early in the morning when the neurologist and her team of residents arrive—jaws on the floor— and there's this breathless lady staggering towards them with this pyscho grin, which is a grin that I would like to call a screw-you grin, but in truth is more like a send-me-home-so-I-can-work-on-my-potted-plants-and-walk-in-my-neighbourhood grin.

The hospice arrangements are cancelled, and she's out there on good old Capilano Crescent in the snow doing laps. Neighbours' heads peer out through curtains, faces brightening in relief—because there's that bloody walking lady, and the world makes sense to them for a few minutes. Because she's walking and smiling, and nothing is as straightforward and reliable as that smile. Which is not really a Nike smile or a send-me-home smile so much as the smile that could never be contained.

The second:

This is more of a general note about coming to understand how she had spent a life cultivating a proficiency at seeing.

She liked it best when she wasn't the centre of attention, when she could sit back and watch her friends do what they did. When Birgit would bring news—and, yeah, she liked the news, but it was the way Birgit would bring news, like Shaq going over the top in New Jersey, ripping the rim from the backboard then heaving it in the river. When Bill and Leona would break into their exchanges, the ones that Albee so shamelessly steals and inserts into the part of the play that sends mouthfuls of tea out through our noses, making us wonder why we'd even bother with the play. When Sandy and Bobby, and Terry and

Mike elevate the feng shui of the living room by simply sitting—four perfectly juxtaposed postures, facial expressions, and mannerisms— four people who, incidentally, would have to be the last four people you'd want to leave off your crew when taking a yacht into uncertain waters. Jenny, who would tiptoe through the door and bring an aura of peace over the room. And Berryl, who would break through the door like a tornado and bring an aura of peace over the room. Then Bev would bring over her daughter Justice, who would bring the peace crashing to the floor—because who wants peace all the time, right? Sheryl and Gilles would use the eyes in the back of their heads to watch Luke and Dez, who somehow never knocked anything over as they trampled on the peace that Justice had laid waste to on the floor. And John's easy movements would bring that peace back to life. Barb's on the speakerphone from Brisbane. Matt's brought beer! And the Dvorkins have flowers. Charlene, Bunny, Dianne, Johanna, and Susan—the book club—would smash down the door and kidnap her for the afternoon. And all those people who lived too far away to drop by, but said, "Anything .. anything we can do, just ... anything ..." before their voices would trail off. And Nick and Irene, who would never—ever—be anything other than Nick and Irene, because that would keep you going for the week when nothing else would.

Her eyes lit up at the ways of these people. These remarkable people. (Her knack was that she only attracted remarkable people.) She'd shake her head in disbelief—What would such remarkable people be doing in MY living room?

The third:

A quick one. After GBM has been stable for a year, she is told that it is growing out of control again, that her time is now very limited. She tears up for, maybe, ninety seconds, has a stiff chai at her favourite coffeehouse (because brandy would interfere with the anti-seizure meds), and sighs "Oh God" once, then signs up for Level I Spanish classes.

This is human temerity.

This is how it is possible to live and die at the same time. And not really die.

The term grace is one of those terms that confound me. It's been expropriated to mean something that I've never quite understood. It seems, at once, to be inadequate, yet totally adequate.

She was the type of person who is a good listener. She learned it from her mother, and in turn has taught her daughter, who has since taken listening to yet another level. Too many people brag about being that person, the one who is a good listener that others come to with their problems. Nobody who ever makes that claim is anybody I would ever take a problem to. She never claimed anything, of course, only waited for them to come. Then listened. Her eyes would blink between states of absolute wonder and absolute knowing. It didn't matter if your life had just fallen apart, or if the schmuck son was going on about Butch Cassidy and a trip to Bolivia. Your story mattered. She'd probe. She'd understand. She'd make you feel like the most important person on the face of the earth because, if only for the time it takes to drink a cup of tea or chat on the phone, you were understood. She never attempted to solve anything. She was empathy, and empathy was the point. Consequently, she brought out the best in anyone who met her. If you liked yourself even a little bit, you wanted to hang out with the lady.

It annoyed me—someone who collects stories for a living—how effortlessly she could get to the bottom of yours with no apparent effort. Unless you've tried to do this yourself—like really do it—then you'll never appreciate the outstanding effort something like this takes. To watch anyone who has perfected anything—like F. Scott Fitzgerald, Bill Gates, Christopher Columbus, Wayne Gretzky, or a granny from the old country making goulash—it seems effortless. Virtuosity is the art and science of making the extraordinary appear ordinary. Her capacity was to live beyond what is known as living passionately, to make compassion what should be expected. And maybe that is also what grace is. The smile that means what is happening matters. That life matters.

Grace is what is done despite every outward sign that doing it would be futile.

I used to wonder what kind of self-hatred it must take to practise the kind of medicine where you already know the outcome of every patient you will treat. To spend your days dealing only with goners. To go to bed at night so numb from the futility of the day's work as to be half-dead yourself.

Her medical team consisted of: a pair of neurosurgeons on opposite ends of the planet; a radiation oncologist whose ear-to-ear grin gave hers a run for its money; a world-renowned neuro-oncologist who never failed to blow you away in the clutch; a palliative doctor whose name wasn't the only part of his character that sounded like "love"; and too many registered nurses and aides who gave more—who were more—than I am capable of describing in anything less than a ten-volume manifesto. These are the people—nurses, doctors, the dozens who fill in the gaps— the ones who rip kitchen sinks from the wall. They are the ones who have driven GBM to its most indestructible forms. The ones who will one day biologically push GBM past all it knows how to cope with.

Of this I have no doubt.

They will do this, not out of self-hatred, but because they are relentless in their belief that life matters. They will do this because there are people like her who somehow hold that belief even more strongly than they do. Something always twigged for them whenever she walked into their waiting room, and they always started to say she's different—but then scrambled to take it back, because their training has taught them to think that everybody's different. Except then she'd walk back in, round after round, with that goddamn smile until finally they just said, "Okay, okay, she really is different." Because she validated the most profound depths of their belief.

When they push GBM past all it knows how to cope with, they will spike it with a small measure of her to make sure it's down.

To be honest, it's difficult for me to be sad. I've teared up about a hundred times—I tear up whenever I think about the fridge or Level I Spanish—but that's not sadness. I tear up when my friend Anik rode her bike around South India, looking for an auspicious place and a Brahmin priest to say a puja. (And if you don't believe in that sort of thing, I'll tell you that a puja was said the same night she sprang up on the eighth floor and started doing laps.)

It's not sad like it is in the movies when people die with so much regret. It's that stupid joy of seeing and realizing that her life has so viscerally touched so many people. That her life has amounted to something. That it is spreading. This is a paradoxical, but very perfect emotion for me. I think it happens like this when one glimpses the illusion of immortality. And in the end, I think that's enough—the illusion.

I teared up when I talked with friends on the other side of the country, too. The ones she has never even met call dutifully at first—but it's mostly for my benefit, to see how I'm coping. "You don't have to phone, you don't have to pray," I lecture. But they only phone more frequently, and I tell them, "Look, there are worse things happening all over the world—please, worry about those things."

But they insist.

And then I realize.

This lady they've never met—they don't necessarily feel bad for her, they feel bad about the way life is. They are inspired by her. This dying librarian who likes to garden. Who has embraced life instead of death.

"Maybe I could drop by some time . . . " Shannon starts once when we've been up all night drinking red wine on opposite ends of the country.

"You don't have to," I emphasize.

There is a long moment of silence.

"It would only be for a minute . . . please? It would be an honour."

And tears would start in my eyes. Because Hall-of-Famers blow free throws in the clutch and celebrities can't sing a song and famous thinkers are famous only because they mock new ideas and the world is run by egomaniacs instead of statesmen. These are the times that Shannon and I live in—we drink so much red wine because we are so let down. But there are other ways to see all around us, and so then we are let down because we drink so much red wine.

Other friends—even now—come to me and insist: "Why her? She was too young, her soul too beautiful. How is this fair?" And I agree with them, but not because it's "not fair." Because not only did she master what it means to inhabit human life—to fully realize life—but she also taught those she loved the trick.

She woke up in the morning and filled her belly with fresh fruit. For a while she had been putting it all into a blender. Washed it meticulously, chopped it meticulously, then—at my urging—liquefied it into something that was no longer whole. Until one day, she said screw that and went back to eating it whole again. She beamed when she ate fresh fruit.

The palliative doctor came by to check her over that morning. I wasn't there, but can imagine the visit. Halfway through, the doctor realized they had a mutual acquaintance—through the library (which is no surprise). But then a deeper flash of recognition occurred. The doctor suddenly realized who this lady really was. The lady who gives comfort but seldom seeks it. The librarian. The Australian. With the garden. Who likes cold, plank-hard vegemite toast. Known by friends of friends and sometimes their friends. That lady doing all that walking. The doctor suddenly blurted out: "My God, you've got strong legs."

One of those dead philosophers said that you can have a kid or plant a tree or write a book. He should have said "and" instead of "or."

And he should have said something about walking.

Their walks were between forty-three and forty-seven minutes long. Some mornings they were longer. Others, less. Up and down hills; rain, snow, hail—all those pony express insurmountable scenarios—my parents always walked. They'd make their rolling observations about the neighbourhood—their piece of the universe—and between both of them, left foot, right, left and right again, she empathizing, he, her long-lost other half, contextualizing the empathy, both revelling in having it all licked. When you were walking, it was all licked. And we'd always take their walking for granted. We don't anymore, of course—right down to the torrid swing of the arms on the upstride.

The most important thing we learned from the walkers is their practice of shared grace. That it didn't have to be cruel or complicated; the walkers never let it be so. There was never any fixed destination when they walked, the point was only to walk and be happy to do so. Left and right, and left and right. Every breath, every step, every movement and thought a way of conveying the big forever, the forever that only ever happens when two people create something more eternal than each could do individually.

That is my context for dropped jaws and twenty laps around the eighth floor at four in the morning with a fridge full of cooking waiting at home.

To the three noteworthy things I should add a fourth. I know she won't like me sharing this last one, but you need to know it.

Near the end, her younger sisters come from Australia, and the three of them break into a crying session. An epic crying session. Which gives way to an epic giggling session, which erupts into such deep laughter that her pants soon become wet. Which, of course, only brings more laughter and more wetness. And more wetness still. Think about this for a second. She laughed so hard she wet her pants. How much more thoroughly can a human feel a moment than to let it trickle down her leg?

And I know she won't like me mentioning that it wasn't even the first time such laughing and wetness happened during her fifty-seven years. She won't mind me mentioning these times either because one day, God willing, you or I might laugh so hard as to pee our own pants, and she'll like the idea that we'll immediately reference her when this happens.

In the end—and this is something you should think about first thing in the morning when there's something to be done about it, rather than late at night, because the end can arrive at any moment—I have learned that grace comes down to how much you are willing to succumb to a pointless moment. With laughter or tears, a stiletto full of piss—it doesn't matter what you succumb to, be it taking a week to nail every last clue on the Boxing Day Crossword, or talking to strangers on the train, or starting on a long brisk walk up lots of hills—simply address the thing that is nagging as you read right now—or at least pause for a moment and acknowledge that there is that thing. And that you'll set out on it this afternoon.

When she first heard about GBM and didn't know what it meant, I hugged her the best that I'm confident I've ever hugged anyone or ever will. Because I knew what GBM meant. By the way that I hugged, she then knew, too. I had wanted to comfort her, but in an instant she realized that I simply had no will to let go. Every part of me was

broken—the only moment of such total breakage I've experienced—
and I realized that I wasn't the one hugging, but the one being hugged.

This is living from dying, which has nothing to do with GBM.
Because this was the concentrated way she lived her entire life.

So I guess you probably already understand that first paradox, the
multiforme reaction of Helen Marie Koentges, HMK. I'll set it down
here for good, nonetheless:

As she lived six times longer with GBM than what is supposed to
be "average," HMK mutated. She glowed and laughed and walked and
worked in a garden that would die in the autumn. As she did these
things, the impact of her existence, via the motley lives of those she
gathering around her, mutated in a way that can only be quantified and
tracked by the expression: "negates the prognosis." Friends, and friends
of friends, dropped by to take her with them, and while she struggled
to beat back GBM on one small area of her brain, the force of her life
swirled. The resistance swelled. A smile and calmness shrouded her until
her very last breath. With a cheeky wink and shrug, she out HMKed
GBM. And now it—and its multiple forms—are dead, while her ashes
are in her garden. And we walk with her grace.

The number of points Gretzky amassed in his career is 3,239. There
are 182 pages in Scribner's edition of *The Great Gatsby*. Columbus
discovered America in 1492. This year, *Forbes* magazine valued Bill Gates
at $58 billion. And none of it inspires me anymore because in the end
she has taught me better.

What is inspiring?

Some time back, when I took to my stool, ordered stout, and my
friend asked the question he would always ask, "How's your mom?" I
answered "You know, it's the last thing I would have thought I'd say in
a million years. I'm embarrassed to even say it like this right now . . .
this-this-this, you know, middle-aged librarian, who gardens and reads
and goes for walks—Christ, man, my MOM, you know, has become
. . . " He ducked his head a little as I whispered the last bit. He thought
about it for a few seconds, then nodded slowly to indicate that it's not
entirely weird that a guy's mom could also be that. And I asked: "How's
your fiancée?"

"She's tough."

Shortly after my mom died, I finished Level I Spanish. There was
borscht in my freezer. Her garden bloomed again that spring. And a few
days from now, when I walk to meet my friend for another beer, I will go
the long way. Always life must pass through death. And by that I don't
mean what you think I mean. Or maybe I do.

LAST RITES

Anita Lahey
Maisonneuve

Over toast, oranges, and oatmeal, Sister Ghislaine, Sister Estelle, and Sister Marguerite cheerfully rehash the latest episode of quiz show *Tous Pour Un*. They wear modest skirts, unwrinkled blouses with vests, and crosses on long silver chains.

Last night's contestant deftly fielded obscure questions about Canadian film—but it wasn't just his intellect that impressed them. When I ask whether he was old or young, Sister Gishlaine's eyes light up.

"Oh, c'était un beau jeune!"

The others nod enthusiastically.

In an alcove stands a sculpture of Marguerite d'Youville, who founded the Grey Nuns in 1737 and, a few years later, was providing soup to the needy in this very room. The original stone hearth still dominates the decor, but nowadays the sisters employ cooks and fetch their meals from the cafeteria-style kitchen on plastic trays.

This light-hearted chat takes place a couple of hours before a funeral, the fifth here in two weeks. Sister Germaine Lalande, ninety-two, died on the weekend, sixty-seven years after joining the convent; she left behind notes thanking Jesus for her childhood among thirteen siblings and the companions she found throughout her life. A sixth funeral will follow soon for the versatile Sister Elisabeth Lafontaine, ninety-four, who died yesterday morning after holding jobs, since 1940, as a teacher, nursing assistant, and librarian.

Everyone here must feel these losses in some measure; it's a small community. But there is no pall over the breakfast table, no weeping in the hallways, no rehashing of these women's final moments. The serenity is not exactly surprising: God's will, "a better place," and all that. But for the Grey Nuns of Montreal in the early twenty-first century, with each individual death creeps closer a larger, more final, demise.

The order got its start when the young Marguerite d'Youville's bootlegger husband died, leaving her with several children and deep in debt. Instead of remarrying, she began taking in those even more unfortunate than herself, and soon amassed a small crew of followers. When the General Hospital in Old Montreal, a home for elderly men and boys, fell into bankruptcy, d'Youville and her team took over. They arrived with a blind woman and a paralyzed widow, instantly broadening the mission's scope. Under d'Youville's watch, the hospital land was cultivated for food; wounded soldiers were admitted, nationality notwithstanding; and "fallen women" and orphans of both genders were given shelter. After d'Youville reportedly discovered a stabbed infant in the river, the sisters established the first foundling hospital on the continent. Despite some head-butting with local authorities— "fallen women" were hardly a popular civic cause—their mission was soon recognized by the King of France and, in 1871, the group officially became a religious community.

At its height in the 1950s, The Sisters of Charity (Les Soeurs de la Charité), more commonly known as the Grey Nuns (Les Soeurs Grises), exceeded 2,000 nuns. By 1981, that figure had dropped below 1,300. Since the passing of Sister Cécile Roussel on August 11, 2006, the Grey Nuns have counted fewer than 500; when this article was completed they had fallen below 440. Their average age exceeds eighty; four are centenarians. The pattern won't change. While a handful of women have joined the fold in South America, no one has taken perpetual vows in Canada since Sister Isabelle Couillard—at forty-two, the youngest Grey Nun in North America—took hers in 1990.

Bittersweetly, 1990 was also the year that d'Youville was canonized, becoming Canada's first native-born saint. Her official list of causes includes single mothers, victims of unrequited love, people butting up against church authorities, people with in-law problems—my favourite!—and parents who have lost a child.

In the coming decades, her sanctified connection to the downtrodden is all that shall remain of the Grey Nuns. For the first time in 270 years, Montreal—a city where pairs of women in grey habits were once a common sight on the bustling avenues—will be a city without a single *soeur grise*.

Not only do the sisters acknowledge this fact, they are fully engaged in the tasks their diminishment entails, from hardcore budgeting and real estate divestment to the solemn ceremonies of the grave.

Amidst this melancholy business, I've been granted permission to bunk for a few nights in the petite maison (little house)—officially known as Maison de Mère d'Youville—the order's original seventeenth-century grey stone residence on St. Pierre Street in Old Montreal. It houses twenty nuns, a few tenants, the congregation's headquarters and archives, and a museum. The order's main Montreal residence is the enormous motherhouse on René Lévèsque Boulevard—a triple-winged giant built by the expanding order in the late nineteenth century, and recently sold to Concordia University for $18 million. For now, it remains home to the bulk of the city's remaining Grey Nuns: about 175 retirees and infirmary patients.

Life for the handful of sisters at the petite maison entails a good deal of travel to and from the motherhouse, and not just for funerals. While I stay here, in a room that consists of a single bed, a desk, a sink, a side table, an antique dormer window, and, of course, a crucifix, I'll be trucking to and fro myself. The idea is to take part in the sisters' daily routine: sharing meals, attending prayer services, and the like—but what it really means is intruding on their quiet extinction; watching them as they watch each other fall away from this world.

The Sisters are making fun of each other for my benefit. "They go early so they can socialize with their friends," one nun says, grinning.

It's 6:30 p.m. A group has congregated to carpool to the motherhouse, where the prayer vigil for the grateful Sister Lalande begins in an hour. A likeness of Mère d'Youville hangs above a workbench in the garage, the same bright-eyed image that appears in every room here. I remark on this to the adventurous Sister Nicole Fournier, the congregation's secretary-general, who taught in the hills of Cameroon and also spent two decades running a mammoth soup kitchen for down-and-out men in the heart of Montreal.

Sister Fournier tells me that the images are meant to bless the space, in particular to protect it from fire. In 1765, after a fire destroyed much of the petite maison, Mère d'Youville boldly declared that they would rebuild, and that the place would never again succumb to flames. (So far, so good.)

This will be my second trip to the motherhouse today. The adventurous Sister Fournier and I took the short drive together this morning, quickly traversing the dozen city blocks. Back when the motherhouse was built, this would have been a long trip to the outskirts of the growing city. It was 1861, and annual flooding had forced the sisters to abandon the petite maison. Having outgrown the place anyway, they went all out on their new digs, hiring prominent Montreal architect Victor Bourgeau and overseeing the construction of an 84,000-square-foot neo-classical, five-storey, grey limestone structure, with a central spire and fifteen-foot ceilings. It spanned an entire city block. Inside were dormitories, a chapel, kitchens, refectories, infirmaries, recreational rooms, parlours, oratories, and offices—not to mention a dental office, pharmacy, printing and binding workshop (for hymn and catechism books), and a workshop for the manufacture of candles and wax statues of the Virgin. An instant landmark, it was depicted on postcards and received guests such as the Governor General of Canada, the Marquis de Lorne. By 1905, the motherhouse's population had swelled to 324 nuns, 340 orphans, 52 abandoned infants, 60 girls, 185 elderly, 26 boarders, and 33 male employees—more than 1,000 residents all told.

An auspicious early history, but these days the place feels, essentially, like a hospital. When Sister Fournier and I arrived this morning, the 10 a.m. mass was underway. Aides and nurses in blue scrubs walked the halls while many of the sixty infirmary occupants sat up in bed, watching the priest on closed-circuit TV. Their names on letter boards called up long-ago worlds in far-flung Quebec villages: Yvette, Georgette, Bibiane, Bernadette, Pierrette.

We waited out the mass and then knocked on the door of Sister Marguerite Daoust. Although she's ninety-two and suffering from health problems, the dogged Sister Daoust was at her desk composing an obituary for the versatile Sister Lafontaine, one of the week's two deceased.

Eyeing a tree outside her window, Sister Daoust told me she meditates on the leaves' annual cycle to help her accept her move to the infirmary. She's entering winter, she said, the "compost" state, the "seed of life." She sent me away with her Saint Thérèse prayer card, insisting on handing it over though she had worn away part of the image on the front with kisses.

Downstairs, over coffee in the refectory, a spacious hall with arched windows, Sister Fournier told me how different things were in the 1960s. During meals, one sister would sit on a raised chair and read scripture: no speaking was otherwise permitted. The sisters used to go to mass together before breakfast; nowadays, they choose a service that suits their schedule, or none at all. They also still wore the grey habits—but this changed in 1968, after Vatican II. Fournier was twenty-seven years old and recalls being thrilled: "the material was hot and heavy." What's more, "people looked at you as part of the group, rather than who you were."

Fournier, now sixty-six, is one of the more youthful in the fold, with dark brown eyebrows against fair features. Originally from La Chute, sixty-five kilometres northwest of Montreal, she joined the order at eighteen, inspired by the communal life and by what she calls, in French, the *audace* of Marguerite d'Youville, whose feminist qualities are highlighted in a pamphlet the nuns distribute. She "stood in opposition to society," it reads; she "rebelled"; she held positions previously reserved for men. What struck Sister Fournier was this: "It would have been rough for a woman at that time to be free enough to say, when her husband died, 'I won't get married again. I want to live by myself taking care of my children.'"

Fournier took her final vows in 1962, and left Quebec soon after to teach French in Cameroon. During her years in Africa, the secularization of Quebec society, better known as the Quiet Revolution, occurred, culminating in the state's wholesale takeover of schools, hospitals, and orphanages. The Grey Nuns' former school for the blind, The Nazareth Institute, is now the government-run Nazareth and Louis-Braille Institute. The Marguerite D'Youville Institute for Nursing is now part of the medical faculty at the Université de Montréal. And so on. When Fournier returned, the nuns were, at least, still operating the soup kitchen Acceuil Bonneau. She took the helm and stayed put for twenty-two years.

Meanwhile, secularization led to a dramatic drop in new recruits, irrevocably sealed in the early 1990s more than 3,000 former wards of the state, the Duplessis Orphans, began demanding compensation for their treatment in Catholic-run institutions forty years earlier—when many were falsely labelled psychiatric patients and allegedly subject to abuse, electroshock, and even lobotomies. Though not directly involved, the Grey Nuns were caught in the broad wave of suspicion against all formerly powerful and influential religious groups.

Perpetually diminishing numbers forced the sisters to continue handing over operations, including those outside Quebec, in western Canada, the north, and in the north-eastern US, a process they have systematized by bringing lay people onto their boards and embarking on transitional partnerships with nonprofit groups and government agencies.

Simultaneously, they are shutting down houses as the groups of sisters who live in them become too small. Among these is the motherhouse itself. The adventurous Sister Fournier walked me out of the refectory and down a long, sunlit hallway with a polished maple floor. She tried the door at the end. It didn't budge.

"Behind this," she said, "are the students."

It was the door to the west wing, the part of the building that, since the sale to Concordia, has been transformed into a student residence. The section is secured by this door from the sisters' quarters. Outdoors, an iron fence does the trick. The two groups enter the building from opposite ends of the property: the nuns off Guy and the students off St. Mathieu.

The locked door may keep students from snooping, but it also bars the sisters from hallways and rooms they have used for generations. Soon other doors will be locked. In 2011, Concordia will claim the chapel and central wing, including a basement crypt that contains the remains of more than 200 of the earliest Grey Nuns. In 2018, the wing that connects to Guy Street goes. As of 2022, the Faculty of Arts and Science takes the entire building. All remaining nuns will then relocate to where it all began: the petite maison on rue St. Pierre, which was reclaimed in the 1980s after existing for more than a century as dock warehouses. Aside from their cemetery at Chateauguay, this will be the last property the sisters own.

Here is where the nitty-gritty work of winding down the organization will be completed, and is already well underway. I spent part of the afternoon here with François Nadeau, one of five full-time archivists whose job it is to organize the congregation's records, going back to the start. These include stacks of rare books; daily handwritten journals; files on living and deceased nuns containing everything from their application forms to personal correspondence; and albums showing photos of nuns making artificial flowers, operating massive laundry wringers, and posing among Inuit and polar bears.

Nadeau, thirty-something, neatly dressed, claimed that things would fall to ruin when his elderly boss, a walking repository of Grey Nuns history, retired; but Nadeau seemed to know a good deal himself. He showed me the boxes in his brickwalled office filled with archival material that has been making its way here from ceased operations. He has to root through every file, decide what's worth keeping, and catalogue it. While we talked, someone wheeled in a cart loaded with yet more boxes. Nadeau looked unfazed.

Meanwhile, one floor down, Sister Faye Wylie, the treasurer, was crunching numbers. "We don't want to take all the money we've saved for charitable purposes and use it to take care of our big buildings and ourselves in our last days," she told me when we met over dinner. She, too, appeared unfazed, even as she described the financial considerations that led to the sale of the motherhouse—it cost a whopping $8 million a year to operate—and her actuarial figuring of rising costs as the sisters age. "This isn't new to us. When the sisters were younger and going to school, that was expensive too." Back then, though, many sisters brought home salaries. Now, aside from donations and seniors' pensions, the congregation has no income.

But the nuns aren't just preoccupied with archives and expenses. Mère d'Youville's stern eyes seem to follow us as we leave the garage in ⸺ of the congregation's immaculate cars, en route to the prayer vigil ⸺ateful Sister Lalande. The sisters are quiet as we travel the dark

I bump into the dogged sister Daoust in front of the coffin. She takes me by the arm. "So you have come to see this."

"Yes."

We regard the casket, in which Lalande's body lies dressed in a beige skirt suit with vest, a rosary of black beads wound around her hands. Her trim, pale face against the white linen appears restful, much younger than her ninety-two years. Yet another sculpture of Mère d'Youville—here she holds a bowl and spoon and is surrounded by children—looks on. Lalande's family is gathered in several chairs to our right. Behind us, more than 200 nuns are seated in folding chairs, some with walkers and canes. "I was here at 1:30 to receive her," says Daoust. "And again at 4:30 for vespers. We don't let her alone."

That said, many of the sisters here tonight will pass on tomorrow's funeral. I'll follow their example, and go instead to Accueil Bonneau, where, from 10 a.m. to noon, I will help serve a hot beef stew, green salad, and bread to more than 400 men. Admitted in waves of a few dozen at a time, they'll eat quickly at long tables, talking little, and then leave. It seems fitting that Accueil Bonneau—with its meals, its clothing depot, its counselling, and the rooming houses it runs with the Montreal Development and Housing Society—is the last major public program in the sisters' care. This is old-fashioned, hardcore, front line social service, exactly how the Grey Nuns got going.

Placing full, steaming bowls before men young and old, I find it uncomfortable to consider the unceremonious takeover of the sisters' works by government, not to mention the animosity levelled at religious orders in the wake of the Duplessis scandal, and now, their careful planning to manage their own care in old age. In a city where they once provided this care for society at large, they have been left to fend for themselves.

The sisters think about this too. My last visit to the motherhouse will entail a chat with the frank Sister Estelle Mitchell, the congregation's spry, ninety-two-year-old resident historian. In the early 1960s, she worked at La Crèche, where more than 700 orphans and foundlings were cared for by Grey Nuns, each sister charged with 20 to 30 children. It's easy to imagine how things might have gotten out of hand in such an environment. Not according to Sister Mitchell, however: "I was three years at La Crèche and if I'd seen one sister hit a child that poor sister wouldn't have survived. We were not told to deal with children like that. We were substitutes for their real mothers."

Nonetheless, she's keenly aware of the mistrust of her kind that exists. Once she facetiously played along with a man who came to her, accusing the sisters of hoarding their assets. "He said Canadian Steamship Lines belonged to the Grey Nuns. I said yes, and also CPR, CN, Radio-Canada. He looked at me like I was crazy. And I said, well that's as true as what you said to me. Would you like to see my bank account?" She smiles at the astonishment on my face. "It doesn't hurt because we know it's not true. It doesn't drive us to despair."

In the end, what would drive the nuns to despair? Here I am, on the last night of my convent sleepover. A candle glows on a small wooden table beside the casket. Women approach in pairs or alone, some bending down to pray, some standing with bowed heads. I ask the dogged Sister Daoust if she knew Lalande well.

"Oh yes. I saw her the day before she died. When I was there she suddenly cried, 'I want to see my mother.' The poor thing. She was so weak, so old."

The vigil is brief. The "Our Father" is recited. One sister reads from the "Letters of Paul to the Thessalonians." Another shares the bare bones of Lalande's life story: her childhood; her entry into the convent; her missions in Quebec, Ontario, Manitoba, and Montreal. A message of consolation from the Superior General, then the "Hail Mary." Finally, "Rendez grace au Seigneur" is softly sung.

As we walk down the aisle I say to Daoust, "It's sad."

This morning she told me none of this was too distressing. "The church was around long before the Grey Nuns were here, and it will continue long after."

But now, as our eyes meet, she reaches for no consoling words, no expression of faith.

"Yes," she says. *"C'est triste."*

THE NEW FACE OF PORN

Alison Lee
This Magazine

The first time I remember thinking critically about pornography, I was fifteen. It was the early 1990s, and my friend and I were going through a stack of discarded magazines, undertaking the well-loved teenage art of collage. Between the *Cosmos* and *National Geographics* was this out-of-place porno, just stuck in there. We made awkward jokes while flipping through it, and found a fake advertisement for "Gash Jeans," which depicted a naked woman bent over with her pants around her ankles. We added it to our collage, and next to it scrawled our own teenage thoughts about porn and sexism.

I'd seen porn before, having snooped through friends' parents' stashes or the collections kept by families I babysat for. But this was the first porn I remember laying eyes on after learning about feminism. Inspired by the punk-feminist Riot Grrrl movement of the early '90s, I took books out of the library by feminist thinkers such as Andrea Dworkin, Catherine McKinnon, and Robin Morgan, whose statement that "pornography is the theory, rape is the practice," summed up the attitude of many feminists of the previous generation.

By the time I found feminism, and started organizing rock shows featuring female artists and making zines, the anti-porn stance had fallen out of fashion in academic circles. But my local public library wasn't exactly on the cutting edge of feminist theory—the information I had access to uniformly condemned pornography as an industry that fed male depravity and encouraged violence against women. Growing up on the bridge between second- and third-wave feminism was a puzzling thing. I revered the anti-porn feminists who gave me my early education in women's studies—they knew, like I did, that women were being systematically harmed, and that it had to be stopped. At fifteen, I thought that watching porn made you hate women.

By sixteen, I wasn't so sure. Younger feminists were taking a broader view of sex and sexuality, including a more open attitude toward porn. Third-wave feminists were more concerned with fighting for sex workers' rights than condemning pornography as a whole. While these schools of feminism weren't mutually exclusive, I had a hard time holding them both in my head without it raising significant questions. Was I supposed to support the hardworking woman in front of the camera, or feel repulsed and sorry for her as an exploited sex object? Since that collage-making session, I've looked at a lot of pornography in a lot of different contexts.

I now see porn as a positive extension of human sexual expression, but I still have a lot of questions about big-picture issues around pornography and society. I've searched for answers in a lot of ways: as an undergrad studying sex and gender; as a sex store manager trying (unsuccessfully) to get porn in stock because my female customers demand it; and as a staff reviewer for a website that informed readers about where to get the best quality blowjob videos online.

I've looked critically at sex, society, and porn for years now, and I still maintain that sex is an amazingly telling lens through which to view the world. This continues today, with my work as manager of Good for Her, a feminist sex store in Toronto, where I also organize the Feminist Porn Awards, which honour the hardworking feminists who are revolutionizing the porn industry. If the very idea of someone who cut her teeth on anti-porn theory now handing out butt-plug shaped trophies to pornographers doesn't make Andrea Dworkin spin in her grave, I don't know what would.

Today, one only has to turn on the TV, walk down the street, or type "free porn" into their web browser to see how unsuccessful the anti-porn movement was. Where anti-porn feminists of the past condemned the entire industry—often with valid reasons—their dogmatic view failed to take into account that sexual imagery can be positive, and that porn is sometimes created by people acting of their free will, who feel good about what they do and who hold pleasure in high esteem.

Now there is porn for everyone. Literally. There are websites that have audio recordings describing pornographic websites for blind people (pornfortheblind.org), porn full of saucy deaf people getting it on and using sign language to express their desires (deafbunny.com), and sites that cater to everything from our fear and fascination with Middle Eastern and Muslim women (arabstreethookers.com) to snot fetishes (seriously: see snotgirls.com if you dare). There is now porn about pretty much anything that a person could ever think of in a sexy way—and plenty that most of us would never find erotic, either. And, of course, there is pornography made specifically for women, who, according to a recent survey by Internet Filter Review, visit adult websites at a rate of one for every two men. Looking back to the time when feminists viewed pornography as an instruction manual for the degradation of women, the biggest irony may be that sexually empowered feminist women have gone from being critics of pornography to being major consumers of it. Pornography, like sex itself, is fraught with complexity and contradiction, but the failure of anti-porn feminism was ultimately positive. Out of its ashes came a new culture of porn that is serious and steadfast in its dedication to pleasure and politics.

The mainstreaming of porn, which, as an industry, rakes in billions and billions of dollars a year, is still primarily a male-driven phenomenon. This doesn't mean it's a boys-only club though—sites that cater specifically to women, like hotmoviesforher.com and sssh.com (a reported 70 percent of women keep their use of internet porn a secret), are doing swift business. The very emergence of a category of "porn for women" or "feminist porn" as a respected and understood niche within the mainstream industry means that somebody is paying attention to the demands of women as consumers of porn. As if more proof were needed of pornography's widespread acceptance, supermodel Tyra Banks recently devoted an episode of her daytime television talk show to the subject of women who watch porn, and the merits of mainstream porn versus porn made by, and for, women.

While pornography's normalization is relatively new, anti-porn crusaders have been around for as long as humans have been casting their sexual dreams and desires into images and print. Right-wing and religious groups have been long-standing enemies of pornography and obscenity, their concerns based on morality and fear that porn would cause the downfall of Western civilization by pandering to base desires—which are supposed to be ignored, of course.

During the late 1970s and 1980s, many feminists began to pay attention to pornography with a different focus. They believed that the growth of porn, popularized in film and magazine form, indicated society's growing tolerance for violating women and reducing them to objects. If we are to pick a year when pornography began its rise, 1953 is a solid one. That's when Hugh Hefner founded *Playboy*, which featured risqué pin-up images that actually look pretty quaint by today's standards. The industry didn't take off in earnest, however, until the early '70s and the advent of feature-length porn films. (Until that time, stag reels—short films usually free of much story or context—were kept out of sight in adult theatres or passed from hand to hand by enterprising men.)

Films such as *Deep Throat* and *Behind the Green Door*, both from 1972, sent audiences flocking to theatres. And these crowds were composed of couples and other curious customers, not just stereotypical raincoat-wearing perverts. The sexual revolution, which espoused free love, the Pill, and an increasingly open view of sex and sexuality—from swingers' parties to gay liberation—set the scene for porn entering the mainstream. The truly explosive growth spurt happened in the '80s with the advent of the VCR: home video technology made porn private and easily accessible. Feminists revolted. Influenced by growing feminist academic study of rape, battering, and trafficking in women, community groups sprang up across North America to protest the proliferation of porn and its perceived effects. In 1979, Women Against Pornography (WAP, one of many groups with such acronyms—there was also Women Against Violence in Pornography and Media, and Women Against Violence Against Women), famously began one of the most visible means of anti-porn protest and education at the time. WAP led tours of the traditionally male domains of the sex underground for women, to give them the opportunity to have a first-hand look at sleazy "adult novelty" shops, dirty bookstores, and porn theatres.

Anti-porn activists also circulated petitions, ran slide shows of pornography in consciousness-raising sessions, and actively attempted to shut down theatres and video stores. Their success was often limited, but according to one activist credited only as "R," there was "one video store owner who gave us his fifty-two tapes, and refused to sell porn." Other successes could be measured by "the number of people who turned out in support, by the number of men we stopped from going into the shops, by the amount of media attention we got for our analysis on pornography, by the number of small groups that formed to organize against pornography in their area as a result of contact with us."

The movement was heated and heartfelt. Some anti-porn activists looked to the principles of direct action and engaged in more overt protest. In 1982, a group calling itself the Wimmin's Fire Brigade attempted to simultaneously bomb three Red Hot Video outlets in the Lower Mainland and Victoria, BC. Ann Hansen, a member of the Brigade (who was also a member of the Squamish Five—famous for bombing a Toronto factory that was manufacturing cruise-missile components), claimed the group targeted Red Hot Video because it was selling "very violent pornography." She said the chain's rapid expansion into suburban neighbourhoods was normalizing porn in areas that previously had little access to sexually explicit material.

While not every feminist with concerns about pornography pursued radical direct action, the bombing captured the sentiment of many women at the time. The British Columbia Federation of Women issued a statement the day after the bombings that stated, "Although we did not participate in the fire bombing of Nov. 22, 1982 . . . we are in sympathy with the anger and frustration of the women who did." The views were not uniform, but in broader society, feminism had become synonymous with anti-porn attitudes and activism.

That year marked a turning point for the anti-porn movement. In 1982, Barnard College in New York held an academic conference on the subject of "pleasure and danger." The purpose of the conference was to investigate how to expand the boundaries of women's sexual freedom and desire, while preserving the feminist project of eliminating sexism and violence. Topics for discussion at the conference included "correct/ incorrect sexualities," teen sex, abortion, disability, and race, and some anti-porn feminists attempted to shut it down, believing the presenters to be perverts and sex deviants. One of the organizers of the conference noted that Women Against Pornography were particularly outspoken in their protest of the event, and greeted the more than 800 attendees with leaflets proclaiming the content of the conference as "anti-feminist."

The event marked a pivotal point in the war against pornography, as anti-porn feminists moved their battle from culture to the courts. The terrain shifted from pro- and anti-pornography to pro- and anti-censorship. And it was an enterprising man from Winnipeg who inadvertently set the stage for the battles to come.

In 1987, Donald Butler was arrested on 173 counts of obscenity, just days after opening an adult video and novelty shop. Butler's entrepreneurial zeal (he re-opened the store and then faced further charges of obscenity), convictions, and journey to the Supreme Court of Canada led to Canada's current obscenity laws, which are based on the Butler decision.

That decision was the culmination of years of anti-porn activism and state intervention. The Women's Legal Education and Action Fund played a significant role, and intervened in the Supreme Court hearings to show the harm that came to women from the production of pornography. LEAF's pro-censorship argument was based on the idea that sexually explicit materials were a form of hate speech against women. The group's intentions may have been good, but the law backfired: the first obscenity case following Butler resulted in the banning of the lesbian magazine *Bad Attitudes* because of a story depicting a sexual encounter that started off as non-consensual. The magazine was confiscated from Glad Day bookstore in Toronto in the spring of 1992 and ignited similar problems with other gay and lesbian establishments, most famously with the Little Sister's bookstore in Vancouver, whose war against Canada Customs, and its restrictive policies on importing gay and lesbian material, raged on for more than twenty years.

The unintended effect of Butler turned out to be a disproportionate number of charges against queer artists and representations of queer sex, including bondage and sadomasochism. LEAF may have been attempting to limit exploitative and abusive practices, but that wasn't how the law came to be used in practice. Instead, cops, customs agents, and judges found many aspects of gay and lesbian sexuality to be inherently demeaning and used the law to harass sexual minorities. For example, anal penetration was initially one of the criteria that could have materials banned. Ironically, it was backlash against these kinds of decisions that put feminists on the other side of the censorship debate. In opposition to this increasing reliance on state censorship that many anti-porn feminists were employing, the Feminist Anti-Censorship Task Force formed in 1984. This group, and other feminists, were increasingly concerned that their anti-porn colleagues were acting out of simple prudery and that they were seeing nothing but violence in all depictions of sex, regardless of context. That, in fact, their views had morphed from being anti-porn to anti-sex.

While anti-porn attitudes dominated the late 1970s and early '80s, with little attention paid to expressions and depictions of women's sexuality from a feminist point of view, the rest of the '80s and early '90s became a hotbed of discussion and theory around getting it on. Self-identified feminists were strutting their stuff and actively showing the many different ways that positive, empowered sex could be showcased.

But that's not to say that all porn magically became so enlightened.

After moving to Toronto in 2005 I'd been out of work for almost five months when I found an intriguing help-wanted ad on Craigslist. The company was looking for writers to review adult websites. With a deep breath and undying love of ridiculous situations, I sent my resumé. The company owner explained the site's concept to me a few days later. My job was to give positive reviews of websites to direct online traffic to such enticing sites as Black Dicks, White Chicks and Big Tits, Round Asses.

As someone who strongly identified as a feminist, I knew taking this job did not reflect my politics. I still felt the sharp division between "good" porn and "bad" porn, and this was definitely bad porn. I had no idea what to expect. The offices were nice, and the project was backed by a semi-retired millionaire who fed his love of toned Latino men by starting several small-time softcore gay websites. I expected that the job would be strange, and an experience unlike anything I'd ever done before, and it was. But I wasn't prepared for the overwhelming boredom that awaited me.

A year and a half into the gig, I was closing in on my 1,000th review; it was becoming difficult to differentiate between websites. The names were nearly indistinguishable, the performers generally looked the same, and the content was often not just similar, but exactly the same, just sold under a different title in order to grab customers with an appetite for whatever niche the sites were selling. The work at this point was automatic. I could do it in my sleep: count the videos and photo sets, document the frequency of updates, and offer some kind of snappy line that made yet another mundane site sound sexily appealing.

Generally I didn't feel sorry for the women in these pictures, but to tell the truth I didn't really think of them all that much—the naked bodies blurred together. But then I came across photos of a woman I knew. Her face and naked body brought me back to reality: we'd had drinks together, talked feminist politics. I was shocked by the reminder that these were all real people with jobs that put them in the strangely public/private realm of porn. Viewing this content day in and day out, my desire to learn about porn as a cultural force and to think about it critically had been overrun by my blasé attitude. There was a difference between what I was viewing and the kind of porn that could be empowering and celebrated, and the difference was suddenly glaring.

My time writing about porn sites often left me feeling conflicted— how feminist was it really to be making money off of the labour of (mostly) women? Could I still call myself a feminist if I was looking at naked ladies all day and not using my position to criticize the glaring sexism and racism that I was constantly viewing? I couldn't help but be disturbed by the sheer number of "reality" porn websites that had premises based on the idea of "tricking" unassuming women (who were obviously actresses following a script) into performing sex acts with promises of money or fame or sometimes just rides to their jobs, and then quickly yanking away these opportunities at the end of the scene. At the end of the day, I knew that what I was looking at was fantasy—a world built up of erotic shortcuts created to arouse (mostly) men. I took this job not so that I could call out the fucked-up parts of the industry, but so that I could pay my bills, and gain more knowledge about the wide world of porn.

What struck me most often when looking at these websites was how frequently I was left feeling sad that this was all that men were being offered. In my time working in sex stores, my own personal goal was to crack open the infinite world of sexuality for people, and especially for women, who are the primary clientele of the shops I've worked in.

Seeing the world of Big Porn showed me that not only are women left out, but men are presented with an incredibly bland palate to work from and to mold their own sexuality. I left my porn review gig believing that the world of porn shouldn't be eradicated, but that it should instead live up to the boundless possibilities of the erotic, and that it should, and could, be able to reflect the diverse bodies, desires, and dreams that make up human sexuality.

I'm fortunate enough to be working in a place now where I can more easily reconcile the split between porn and feminism. At Good For Her, a staunchly feminist sex store, I'm partly responsible for stocking our shelves with independent porn (with occasional big studio features) that live up to the promise of erotic materials that address women as viewers.

This spring I organized the third annual Feminist Porn Awards, held in Toronto to recognize filmmakers who are doing it right, showing sex as positive and healthy, with categories such as Fiercest Female Orgasm, Deliciously Diverse Cast, and Most Tantalizing Trans Film. The films all depict consent and active desire, with women as agents of their libidos, rather than being shown as racialized or inferior objects. Leading up to the awards, which attracted an audience of more than 450 women (and even a few men), the bulk of my work hours were spent trying to get the word out—I conducted many interviews with journalists who were confused by the very idea of feminists honouring porn flicks. A healthy part of my day became the Google search, looking for mentions in the media and on blogs. Most of the coverage I found was positive, and the negatives were hard to separate from online trolls looking to bait anyone with a different opinion. But the criticisms that I read most often, primarily on feminist blogs, focused on the impossibility of there ever being any such thing as feminist porn. The belief seems to be that recording a woman in a sex act was inherently degrading; the thought that any woman could choose to star in, or write and direct, her own porn is unfathomable to these critics. For all the problems that mainstream porn presents, I knew that women can—and do—choose to be involved in the industry, either within big productions or in their own indie affairs. I knew this because I'd been talking to many of these women for weeks, and asking them to be a part of these awards. I was talking directly with the vanguard of the new porn revolution.

One such woman is Erika Lust, a thirty-one-year-old mother of an incredibly cute toddler, and a pornographer. When Lust started making films, she wanted to provide something she couldn't find anywhere else—porn targeted at straight women. "I want to make movies for straight girls because we are a big group of people and we are supposed to go with the mainstream heterosexual porn, made by men for men," she says. "Lesbians, gays, trans—every group lately has their own porn, and I felt that nobody was thinking about the needs and desires of heterosexual women. We are supposed to be happy and satisfied with *Sex and the City*, *Desperate Housewives*, or *Playgirl* movies, but we need more than that!"

Her debut film, *Five Hot Stories for Her*, has won multiple awards (including a Feminist Porn Award for Movie of the Year in 2008).

Her latest project is premised on the idea that female audiences want to get to know the subjects they are watching more intimately than standard porn allows for. Barcelona Sex Project shows three men and three women being interviewed and talking about their sexual tastes and fantasies before they engage in some sultry solo sex.

While there is a history of women writing stories and taking pictures and even making movies that have been intended or used to fuel erotic fantasies, it's only been recently that these have been marketed as porn for women. (Exceptions include Candida Royalle, who started in 1984, and is especially well known in the world of porn for women; her softer-focus flicks show female characters that have an equal stake in their sexual encounters.) Women have claimed a share in the means of production in what has traditionally been a male-dominated industry, and they are finding success both in and outside the larger industry. Tristan Taormino, an acclaimed sex-columnist turned director, makes educational titles, such as *Tristan Taormino's Expert Guide to Anal Sex*, as well as racier projects. Her just-released *Chemistry Volume 4: The Orgy Edition* takes six porn stars and puts them up in a house for thirty-six hours, *Big Brother* style, giving them the power to script their own scenes, and take part in the filming as well. The performers get a lot of say in how they want to be represented and exactly what kind of sex they want to engage in.

This is not to say that everything is always perfect in feminist porn land—as has always been the case with feminism, there is never one solid vision of what "feminist" is, and what calling yourself a feminist pornographer really means. And there are disputes. Lust and another female director, Petra Joy from the UK, were involved in a minor skirmish in the feminist porn blogosphere when Joy disputed the application of the feminist label for certain sex acts caught on film: "If you want to show come on a woman's face that's fine, but don't call it feminist," she wrote on her website. Lust took offense to this and shot back a passionate response in her blog, saying she was sad that "certain women devote their time and energy to pulling down the work of other women, instead of focusing on empowering our different approaches and points of view."

While Joy made sure to say she believed that any feminist could show whatever she liked in her films, the sentiment remained that there were, or should be, rules in place. Is showing semen on a woman's body inherently demeaning? If a performer is choosing to engage in these acts, and states either that it doesn't bother her or more, that she relishes it, can we condemn the result?

When I was a teenager making my first dives into feminism, I couldn't always wrap my head around the divides within pornography and notions of sex-positive expression in general. Even now, the call to support sex workers is too often predicated on getting them out of sex work, even if that is where they want to be. The idea that feminism was going to "save" women, either from performing in porn or from experiencing the presumed violent effects of porn still smacks too much of paternalistic control. Women need to be supported in their decisions and choices around sex and sexuality, and that includes appearing on websites some find gross, or checking out porn on cable channels and finding new ideas and acts that turn them on—even if it's porn free of politics.

Anti-porn feminists had (and do have) their hearts in the right place. The problem remains that sex and porn are not inherently bad; it's exploitation, unsafe working conditions, coercion, and advocating violence that are never okay. Feminist porn producers already depict women as active participants in their own sexual fantasy. The project going forward will be to continue to ensure safe, appropriate working conditions for those who appear in and produce porn, while continuing to work on traditional feminist goals, including eradicating the exploitation of women. Erika Lust's film company, for instance, donates five percent of its revenue to Equality Now and Womankind Worldwide, non-governmental organizations combatting sexual exploitation.

On the production side, more women are taking the reigns with distribution, ensuring that they remain in control of how and where their work is displayed. With the success of porn on the Web, performers running their own sites are increasingly able to reap a larger percentage of the profits and maintain creative control in ways that wouldn't be possible in the mainstream.

Feminist porn may not be the answer to all of the critiques of pornography as a genre and an industry, but it is a start that looks to the infinite possibilities the future holds for porn. Access to porn is expanding every day: Canadians will soon have a cable channel with 50 percent Canadian programming—mandated by the CRTC.

Film festivals are popping up from New York to Berlin to showcase erotic work in legitimate venues, and the Feminist Porn Awards are marching into their fourth year. Adult trade magazines are paying increased attention to independent porn marketed toward women, and the mostly-untapped female audience is being specifically wooed more and more.

Consumers have the opportunity to demand better porn, and we are doing just that on a larger scale than ever before. The new face of porn has an opportunity to disrupt stereotypes and address new viewers, all while creating a feminist view of sexuality. As Erika Lust says, "porn and feminism must be allies: they have to fight together against the conservative notion of considering [sex as something] that has to be only related with reproduction, and labeling [sexually] active women as whores. Both feminism and porn can help liberate women from what society expects from us: to be good, quiet nice girls, not complaining, not arguing, not fighting, not enjoying sex, not being powerful and provocative." Women can watch and make porn as a powerful statement against the status quo, one dirty DVD at a time.

THE RETURN OF BEAUTY

Nick Mount
Queen's Quarterly

You find one on Madison Street, near Pike, beyond the shadow of the Manhattan Bridge. It hovers on the wall of a makeshift parking lot, over exhaust, rust, old tags. It shouldn't be here, but there it is—a hummingbird. Lifesize and lifelike, put in flight by the old painter's tricks of shadow and light. You could have thought it real but for its colours, which come from art, not nature—from the graffiti behind it, its backdrop and its ancestor. Its creator says he wants the bird to give pause, and that's just what it does. Give pause. Because here, in an ugly corner of an ugly city, within choking distance of the wreckage of an ugly act, you have found the opposite of ugly. Here, beauty is back.

In 1917, Marcel Duchamp bought a urinal from a New York ironworks, signed it "R. Mutt," and entered it in the exhibition of New York's Society of Independent Artists. And so, the story goes, a toilet conquered the world. In 2004, a poll of 500 artists, curators, critics, and art dealers named Duchamp's Fountain the most influential art object of the twentieth century.

Avant-garde artists like Duchamp refused to produce art for the pleasure of a society they held responsible for, among other things, World War I. They walked away from a definition of art that had ruled the West for over 2,000 years: no more beautiful imitations. Art should be a concept, not a copy. It should disturb, not please. Most important, it should not be beautiful. The American painter Barnett Newman said it clearest: "The impulse of modern art was to destroy beauty."

That's why Duchamp's urinal was the right choice for the most influential art object of our time. There are exceptions, but all it should take is a walk through any major art gallery to convince you that for twentieth-century art, beauty really isn't the point. That's not to say that it's not art, or that it's not good art. In fact, according to the philosopher Arthur C. Danto, author of the best of several recent versions of this story, that was the main insight of modern art: art does not have to be beautiful to be art.

If a trip to the gallery doesn't convince you—if you still say Duchamp's urinal is beautiful, or Picasso's women, or Pollock's splatters, or Hirst's rotting animals—blame your expensive education. In its attempt to explain the value of avant-garde art, art criticism fell back on art's traditional value. Again and again, curators and critics said this new art was beautiful, if we could only open our eyes. Even when their own eyes told them otherwise.

Clement Greenberg, America's most influential modernist art critic, said it more baldly than most: "Pollock's bad taste is in reality simply his willingness to be ugly in terms of contemporary taste. In the course of time this ugliness will become a new standard of beauty."

Greenberg was right—more right than he would have liked, especially as a New Yorker. After September 11, the French philosopher Jean Baudrillard wrote, "By the grace of terrorism, the World Trade Center has become the world's most beautiful building—the eighth wonder of the world!" The *New York Times* called Baudrillard cold-blooded, but Baudrillard wasn't especially cold-blooded, just especially educated. He could call the wreckage beautiful because he had ingested, more thoroughly than most, the modernist lesson that the ugly is beautiful, in its own way.

Beauty had other enemies in the last century besides the avant-garde and Ray Stevens. Feminism attacked the "beauty myth," the reduction of female appearance to a single male ideal. Poststructuralism and multiculturalism chipped away at universals in general, European universals in particular. Art elevated concepts over aesthetics to its logical end: the explicit exclusion of apolitical art from the international exhibition in 1997. In the galleries, ugly was the new beauty. In the classrooms, everyone was beautiful. For good and noble reasons, both. But in becoming anything, beauty became nothing, a word that could describe anything and that, consequently, no one could describe.

Beauty never left, of course. Exiled from high culture, it found a home throughout the century in mass culture, in its movies, magazines, music, advertising. On one side, cubist prostitutes; on the other, Barbies and Britneys. Advertising especially welcomed beauty: its seduction, its youth, its promise of better sex and a better life. Today, Plato's "Symposium" is a marketing manual.

While high art and high theory have never been so sceptical of beauty, daily experience has never been so certain. Countless psychological studies show us agreeing on the most attractive human face, agreement that cuts across gender, class, age, even race. The jury is still out on whether this consensus comes from nature or nurture, survival of the prettiest, or *America's Next Top Model*. But at the very least, global mass culture has refined our everyday taste while high culture has failed utterly to change it. With the best of intentions, the twentieth century surrendered beauty to commerce. For beautiful art, we got beautiful shoes. For beautiful cities, beautiful billboards.

In 1993, the maverick American art critic Dave Hickey surprised the art world and himself by declaring at a conference that "The issue of the nineties will be beauty." The following year, The *New Yorker's* future head art critic, Peter Schjeldahl, wrote a defence of beauty for *Art Issues* that the *New York Times Magazine* later reprinted as a cover story. "There is something crazy," Schjeldahl wrote, "about a culture in which the value of beauty becomes controversial."

So began, or so we noticed, what looks like beauty's return to its old haunts. In 1999, the Smithsonian's Hirshhorn Museum marked its twenty-fifth anniversary with an exhibit called *Regarding Beauty: A View of the Late Twentieth Century*. The years since have seen shows of nineteenth- and twentieth-century art that hasn't been exhibited for decades, or never was: bourgeois Salon painters at Austria's Kunsthalle Krems, the Pre-Raphaelites at Tate Britain, the Nabi painter Maurice Denis at the Musee d' Orsay, Alberto Vargas's pinup girls at the University of Kansas, pages from *Vogue Italia* at the Royal Academy, Norman Rockwell at the Guggenheim.

In the literary arts, similar signs. Literature never rejected beauty as loudly or thoroughly as the visual arts, probably because the dominant literary form of the twentieth century—the novel—felt the tug of mass culture much more than visual art. But it fell into line, for art's reasons and its own. After World War I, being authentic mattered more to writers than being beautiful. Beauty was for the Victorians; we were tougher, smarter, cooler. In its version of art's conceptual turn, literary criticism diminished what beauty remained by preferring ideas to books and picking its books accordingly. Twentieth-century literature didn't fulfill the Dadaist poet Tristan Tzara's desire to assassinate beauty, but only because it didn't care enough to pull the trigger.

But around the mid-1990s, book reviewers suddenly started using the B-word again. So did a few books, like the Canadian poet Anne Carson's *The Beauty of the Husband*, a verse essay that revisits Keats's equation of truth and beauty. Or the American novelist Richard Powers's *Plowing the Dark*, in which an artist who abandoned art because art abandoned beauty gets a second chance. In her book, *Venus in Exile*, the critic Wendy Steiner wrote about seeing a revived hunger for beauty in all five of the shortlisted novels for the 1997 National Book Critics Circle Award. As proof of beauty's return, her discussion isn't terribly persuasive. But as proof of Steiner's own longing as a reader and a critic for these books to contain beauty, to be beautiful, it's completely convincing.

For the moment, that's beauty's most conspicuous return to the high arts: not in art, but in talk about art, exactly where the twentieth-century's injunction against beauty was most dogmatic. In criticism and philosophy, beauty and its attendants—craft, feeling, sincerity, ethics, truth—have become permissible subjects again.

In the universities, the last decade has seen an outburst of conferences, graduate seminars, articles, and books on beauty. Because of the academy's confusion of its responsibility with page counts, it's dangerous to take quantity as a real measure of its interest in anything. But the best of the new work on beauty—like Dave Hickey's *The Invisible Dragon*, Elaine Scarry's *On Beauty*, and Alexander Nehamas's *Only a Promise of Happiness*—seems driven in thought and style by personal and sincere motives. Like Wendy Steiner's attempt to find beauty in the novels she reads, it's born of desire, of the recovered memory that a life without beauty is, as Plato said, not worth living.

Beauty hasn't returned to these scattered fields ironically. It's back sincerely, for its own merits. Beauty is susceptible to irony, a point twentieth-century art proved repeatedly. But beauty is not itself ironic. If you see irony in the beautiful, you brought it there. The incompatibility of beauty with the late twentieth century's affection for irony is one reason it stayed away from the high arts as long as it has. As psychologist James Hillman has said, to bring beauty back, we'll need "the courage to abandon irony."

That momentous swing may have begun. In 1993, the American writer David Foster Wallace argued that the pervasive irony of postmodern culture makes it immune to critique or change by irony. Wallace suggested, audaciously, that the next generation of literary rebels might be anti-rebels, writers who "dare somehow to back away from ironic watching, who have the childish gall actually to endorse and instantiate single-entendre principles." Eight years later, the young British curator Mark Sladen described American artists of his generation as "post-ironic."

And then, September 11. Suddenly, irony was out and sincerity in, from poignant street shrines to stern presidential promises. Suddenly, we were post-postmoderns with a vengeance, entering what *Vanity Fair* editor Graydon Carter called "the end of the age of irony." Maybe, as many said and more blogged, Carter's prediction was premature. But maybe not. Baudrillard's description of the destroyed towers as beautiful marked the culmination of a century of abusing beauty, its insanely sane conclusion. Endings are also beginnings.

Despite 9/11, actual beauty remains rare in actual art. With a handful of exceptions, beautiful imitations still take a back seat to clever concepts, or to other aesthetics, like the sublime and the abject. When beauty does surface, it's still as grist for the concept, the target of a well-educated irony.

Take *Regarding Beauty*, the Hirshhorn's anniversary exhibit. Inspired by Hickey's prediction that beauty would be the "issue" of the 1990s, the organizers placed the weight of their punning title squarely on thinking about, rather than looking at, beauty. In her catalogue essay, co-curator Olga M. Viso claimed that artists no longer shun beauty, that beauty now exists "to be embraced as well as challenged." But in the exhibit itself, challenges far outnumbered embraces. Almost all the pieces continued the attack on beauty, from Andy Warhol's intentionally repetitive *Marilyn Monroe's Lips* in 1962 to Rosemarie Trockel's Beauty in 1995, a series of outdoor posters whose computer-generated "perfect" female faces parody Benetton ads.

Of the three-dozen artists selected for *Regarding Beauty*, only the work of a few—three, by my count—is sincerely beautiful. There is room for disagreement about this, but not nearly as much we've been taught by a century of seeing beauty anywhere. Almost by definition, beauty is what you know, instantly, to be beautiful. Beauty stands out, both from other aesthetics and from lesser versions of itself. Prolonged exposure can deepen or wither your perception of beauty, in a poem or a person, but not the beauty itself, the beauty you saw then. We're not always ready for it, but beauty is immediate.

In the spring of 2007, I taught one of those new graduate seminars on beauty at the University of Toronto. For our final class I asked the students—myself and twenty MA and PhD candidates from the English, Philosophy, and Fine Art departments—to find beautiful art by a contemporary artist. Looking back, we didn't come up with much. Andy Goldsworthy, the well-known British sculptor who makes ephemeral outdoor pieces from natural materials like rocks, leaves, and snow. A young Canadian sculptor, Cal Lane, who cuts delicate, lace-like patterns into everyday metal objects like shovels, oil cans, a wheelbarrow. Recent semi-abstracts by two British painters, Howard Hodgkin and Cecily Brown. In architecture, Studio FAM's glass memorial for the Madrid train bombing, and Foster and Partners's glass-covered court at the British Museum.

We saw others, but these are the few that immediately convinced us of their beauty, that stood out. It's possible that we found so few because we were too ignorant or too educated: that we knew too little about contemporary art, or too much about the pitfalls of beauty. But even granting those problems, I think we found little beautiful art in the real and virtual galleries of the West because there is still little to be found. The month our seminar began, the designer Bruce Mau wrote in *The Walrus* that "Today the talent to make beautiful paintings is a bus pass to the suburbs of art discourse." Add beautiful sculpture and beautiful buildings, and that's pretty much what it took us three months to find out.

In a sense, Mau was wrong. Beauty is closer today to the centre of art discourse than it has been for decades. But in another and more important sense, he's right, more right than I think he realized. Beauty has returned to art, not just to talk about art. It's just that its most vital return hasn't been to the centre of the art world, it's been to its edges—to, quite precisely, the suburbs of art. Today, beauty is using that bus pass.

Dan Witz is one of several artists who have been called the godfather of street art. Witz grew up in Highland Park, a suburb on Chicago's affluent North Shore. He studied at the Rhode Island School of Design in the mid-1970s and in 1980 received his BFA from the prestigious Cooper Union in New York's East Village. As Witz tells the story, he began doing street art while at Cooper, because of Cooper. Rebelling against the school's elitism—"the postmodern architecture, the chilly art snob students"—he got drunk one night and painted fires up and down its back stairway.

Ironically, students at highbrow Cooper taught Witz the lowbrow skill for which he's become known, his ability to paint hyper-realistic images that "trick the eye," *trompe l'oeils*. Witz began fooling New York's eye in 1979 with his first large-scale street project, *The Birds of Manhattan*. Working with tiny brushes and acrylic paint, he painted over forty hummingbirds on walls and doors in Lower Manhattan. Besides the *trompe l'oeil* illusion of three-dimensional realism, Witz used a technique called scumbling—thin layers of one colour over another—to capture the iridescent shimmer of a hummingbird's plumage. The birds are not actual species: Witz let each adapt to its environment, taking its colour cues from the surface on which it flew.

Street art grew from graffiti, but it uses a wider range of techniques and styles. It's more educated: graffiti with a BFA, as its detractors say more often than its defenders. It's less about asserting the self than addressing the world, sometimes through political content, more often through inclusive aesthetics. The most striking difference, the shift Witz anticipated by over a decade, is street art's new permissiveness towards the cute and the beautiful, aesthetics as off limits in graffiti as in the galleries.

In retrospect, *The Birds of Manhattan* was street art *avant la lettre*, two years before Blek le Rat pioneered stencil graffiti in Paris, a decade before Shepard Fairey launched his *Obey Giant* campaign out of a Rhode Island skateboard shop. But at the time, Witz's birds were less street art than art taking to the streets, like Jenny Holzer's *Truisms* of two years before and Keith Haring's subway drawings two years later. Witz assumed his outdoor art would be for him what it became for Haring, Lee Quinones, Jean-Michel Basquiat, and other artists working the New York streets at the same time: a step on the way to the galleries. Throughout the 1980s he worked both sides of the fence, studio painting in the winter and occasional, mostly light-hearted, street pieces in the summer.

In the early 1990s, a motorcycle accident together with Witz's persistent misgivings about the dollar-driven gallery scene forced him to reassess his place in art. In 1994, he recommitted himself to street art with his first major project since *The Birds of Manhattan*, a series of grim, hooded figures postered on walls overlooking heroin spots in his Lower East Side neighbourhood.

Since then, Witz has returned to the streets every summer with a new project. His dominant style remains *trompe l'oeil* realism, though to reduce his exposure to increasingly anti-graffiti New York police he stopped handpainting on site in the early '90s, working instead in the studio with a photograph printed on vinyl sticker paper and painted to add dimension. On site, Witz airbrushes shadows around the sticker, a process that gets him off the street in under five minutes.

Witz employs several aesthetics. *Hoodies* is as dark as its content, heroin and HIV in the Lower East Side of the early '90s. Street art's affection for the cute surfaces in his humour, street pranks like a house he turned into a face by adding a red weather balloon for a nose. But his driving aesthetic is beauty. In 2000, when Witz left his Ludlow loft for Brooklyn, he revived his birds as a farewell to his old neighbourhood. Once again hummingbirds flew in Lower Manhattan, on Madison, on Henry, in Freeman Alley. Back in 1979, Witz looked for clean canvases for his birds, untagged walls and doors. In 2000, he let them fly over old graffiti, announcing the relation and the difference between the two aesthetics, tradition and departure.

The summer after September 11, Witz stuck candlelit shrines on the bases of light poles radiating out along sightlines from Ground Zero into midtown, New Jersey, and Brooklyn. The pieces began as photographs of the votive offerings left in Union Square Park after the attacks, painted in Witz's way to light the night again. New beauty, for an old end: consolation.

The *WTC Shrines* is Witz's favourite work to date, his best marriage of form and function. Mine is *Floating*, a series from 2005 of tiny rowboats set afloat on the sides of dumpsters, trains, tractor-trailers—anything that moved. The boats all have the same name: *Lonesome*. In context, and nowhere else, they are a near perfect image of urban pathos, transient

Prufrocks for the twenty-first century. They hear the mermaids sing, but not for them.

For Witz, public art should be publicly accessible. "My small goal is to give pause, to say art is around, that it is a possibility. I want ordinary people to know that places like this street aren't always what they seem." His aesthetic follows from that goal: beauty is naturally accessible to "ordinary people," which is one reason high art spurned it and the main reason commerce embraced it. Witz's medium might be new, in other words, but his methods are old, pre-urinal. *Trompe l'oeil* dates to the Greeks, to the dawn of beautiful imitations. Scumbling is an Old Masters' technique last used extensively in Impressionism, beauty's last gasp.

Conservative methods do not necessarily make conservative art. Accessibility matters to Witz as a starting point, a way in for all, but he uses beauty not to please but to provoke. Last fall, he wrote me that he chose beauty as "a calculated punk reaction, a form of rebellion, an artist's line-in-the-sand manifesto rejecting boring, elitist, intentionally exclusivist art practices. Beauty as sedition." Outside the art world, Witz's street art is equally radical for the simple, courageous reason that it's free: a public beauty that costs nothing to see, and has nothing to sell.

Witz is not alone. The young New York street artist known as Swoon wheatpastes fragile paper cutouts of her family, friends, and city characters—beauty caught and left to rot. In Montreal, Roadsworth spraypaints ivy along the painted lines on streets, or did until he plea-bargained mischief charges in 2006. Sometimes the beauty of street art is in the content more than the form, as in the hundred-plus "I Love You" tags someone sprayed across Toronto in 2001. Sometimes it's not even in the street: the Wooster Collective, street art's online conscience, claims Andy Goldsworthy as one of their own.

At the moment, the amount of beautiful art is about the same on the streets as in the galleries: very little. But the crucial difference is that while beauty is still largely excluded from or treated as an "issue" by the art world, it's being welcomed on the streets, by Witz's ordinary people. Witz, Swoon, and Roadsworth are not typical street artists, not yet. They're exceptional—and exceptionally admired. And although it's no guarantee, history gets made by exceptions. In 1917, urinals weren't typical art either.

Street art isn't the only artistic suburb to welcome beauty back in recent years. Beauty's back with heels and humour in the neo-burlesque, the revival of American burlesque that began in the mid-1990s. It's back with a tear in its eye in indie music, in the explosion of sensitive singer-songwriters we would have beat with a bat in the crotch-rock

'80s. It's back as a child in so-called Outsider Art, both the unskilled folk art brought inside and the skilled folk art left outside, like the painter Thomas Kinkade calls "America's most collected living artist," i.e., Thomas Kinkade. It's back as craft in border-crossing extensions of punk's DIY aesthetic to the rebirth of vinyl, the Lowbrow movement, Martha Stewart, sculpture's turn to homemade materials, poetry's return to metre and rhyme, art's return to paint.

Some, or all, of these will disappear, passing with fashion or swallowed whole by art dealers and advertisers. The internal backlash against street art has already begun, with accusations flying in paint and words of artists selling out to galleries and corporations as well as charges of white artists stealing a black art, the tired and tiring Elvis story. The New York street art news last summer was dominated by the Splasher, an anonymous artist who's vandalizing the vandals, Pollocking house paint on street pieces by crossover successes like Swoon and Fairey. The Splasher's manifesto quotes Dada scripture, demanding the destruction of all bourgeois art. Old toilets die hard.

Beauty will survive the passing of street art, of any art. If it could endure all we threw at it in the twentieth century, it can handle a little house paint in the twenty-first. In art, beauty is just one aesthetic choice among many. But as Arthur Danto has said and Plato before him, it's the only aesthetic that is essential to life as we would prefer to live it. In the last century, we got our public beauty fixes from nature and commerce, not art. Nature is too far away now, and commerce has another agenda. Beauty's return reveals an enduring hunger for nearby beauty that's not for sale. Kant was wrong: billboards can be beautiful. But they're not enough.

For Danto, beauty has returned to the post-9/11 world because beauty eases pain. It's the appropriate aesthetic for our elegiac mood: candles in the parks, soft ballads by pop gods, Witz's street shrines, the Madrid memorial. We convinced ourselves that beauty was subjective, in the eye of the beholder. But when we needed to come together in the communal rites of mourning and elegy, we chose beauty all the same.

Beauty's use as consolation after September 11 wasn't a movement so much as a moment, one we'd shared many times before in the long litany of twentieth-century pain. We may have snubbed beauty, but we made sure to keep some around for experiences too intense for avant-garde theory to relieve. There are no Damien Hirst reproductions in hospital gift shops.

Beauty isn't back just to help us deal with the past. It's back to help change the present and create a different future. In a poster by Britain's best-known street artist, Banksy, a masked graffiti artist in black and white cocks his arm to throw a bouquet of flowers in full colour. In one of Witz's street illusions, a hand punctures a metal utility box to clutch a single rose. These are not beauty as consolation—they're beauty as provocation, as deliberately seditious as Duchamp's urinal was in 1917. Strange, how far we've come: that flowers could be rebellious.

Beauty has much to offer, starting with the pleasure of seeing it. I enjoy the intellectual delights of conceptual art as much as the next PhD, but after a while (say a hundred years) they can become predictable. Challenging the viewer's definition of art, check. Deconstructing the white cube, check. Exposing the politics of representation, check. Art cannot be blamed for having few new ideas: the number of ideas entering the world at any given time is exceedingly small. But it's not unreasonable to ask it to recognize this limitation, and to aim once in a while at pleasure instead. It's not as easy as it looks, or as simple.

Many of the people who are talking about beauty again are doing so because they believe that besides giving pleasure, pleasurable art can change the world. For the art critic Wendy Steiner and the philosopher Elaine Scarry, for instance, beauty engenders crucial political virtues. For Steiner, beauty invites communication between the beholder and the beheld, the self and the other—the beginnings of empathy and equality. For Scarry, beauty's fragility fosters the desire to protect it, and so might teach us to extend our care from the extraordinary artwork to the ordinary person.

Scarry goes further, standing on Plato's and Kant's shoulders to argue that beauty points the way toward justice itself. It's more than a coincidence, she says, that we describe both beautiful objects and just outcomes as "fair." Beauty's main attribute is justice's main goal: symmetry. But unlike justice, which is necessarily general and abstract, beauty is present to the senses, particular and concrete. In answer to the question "What does a just society look like?" Scarry says we might answer, "like the sky."

I'm not sure beauty can achieve what we could not, or that we should expect it to. In his recent book *Only a Promise of Happiness*, Alexander Nehamas is also doubtful, arguing that beauty offers no moral or social value beyond itself—only the uncertain promise that my life will be better for the time I spend with it. But even Nehamas ends up saying that in an uncertain world, "the promise of happiness is happiness itself." His beauty gives the individual what Scarry's gives the world, a better life for you and me that presumably adds up to a better life for all.

If beauty offers anything beyond pleasure, it's to be found in its much-contested universality. Perhaps we need a safer word: Nehamas suggests communal. But hopefully universal or cautiously common, long experience and recent science show widespread agreement on beauty and its appeal. If it isn't universal, it's the most universal aesthetic we've got. Maybe it's time to admit again what Friedrich Schiller said more clearly than Kant, that "Beauty alone makes the whole world happy, and each and every being forgets its limitations while under its spell."

Beauty's magic can of course be used for unhappy ends. Mass culture's embrace of beauty doesn't necessarily make its products good for us. Beauty works as well to foster the warrior spirit as it does to lament its leftovers, from Rupert Brooke's beautiful poems in World War I to Silvia Pecota's beautiful pinups for the Canadian troops in Afghanistan. But in a time scarred by the differences among us, anything that can remind us of our similarity without erasing our differences has tremendous political potential for good. Beauty doesn't get to decide for whom it works. But we do.

In his defence of beauty back in 1994, Peter Schjeldahl suggested that maybe we banished beauty because we couldn't forgive it for not saving the world. But we never gave it a chance: we hid its survivors in museums and mansions and sold its public space to the advertisers. We don't actually know what an ethical beauty could do if we let it loose in the world, because we haven't tried. As Dan Witz says of his form of public art, "Not for sale is the most radical thing to happen in art since abstraction."

Some believe ethics must come before beauty, the no-poetry-after-Auschwitz school. Duchamp, for starters: no more beautiful art for an ugly world. The Splasher, for another: "OUR STRUGGLE CANNOT BE HUNG ON WALLS. DESTROY THE MUSEUMS, IN THE STREETS AND EVERYWHERE." Less typographically excited but just as certain, Danto says beauty cannot return to art until politics ends injustice, while Peter Schjeldahl calls beauty "a necessity that waits upon the satisfaction of other necessities."

They're probably right. Art isn't water, it's wine. But I like wine. The problem with putting politics before beauty is that it makes beauty contingent upon utopia, and I can't wait that long. Until the Marxists make the world perfect, perhaps the rest of us can make it a little better, a little fairer, and a little happier—with the help of Dan Witz and Swoon, and, yes, Martha Stewart and Thomas Kinkade.

Beauty is not all there is or should be. I don't want to live inside one of Kinkade's bucolic paintings, and not just because I'd burn in his utopia. The human range of emotions deserves a range of aesthetics: it would be a mistake to abandon everything art learned in the twentieth century, just as it was a mistake to abandon everything it learned about beauty in the centuries before—the skills we replaced with theories. Nor is the beauty of the beautiful the end of the story: to call an artwork beautiful does not say all there is to say about it, any more than it says all there is about a person. And nor, finally, are beautiful shoes without their pleasure or virtue. Soweto's new malls are better than its old shanties—not perfect, just better.

But while we're waiting on utopia, beauty could do this imperfect world some good. Especially in public spaces, beauty could bring us together, remind us of what we share—in times of joy as well as grief. It could win our attention back from commercial beauty, showing us other pleasures besides shopping, other ways to see and think about our bodies, our values, our cities. Maybe, just maybe, it could point the way toward a fairer politics as well as a fairer home. And even if beauty can't do those things—even if it can't make the world we want—it can certainly make it easier to live with the world we have.

We don't just like beauty, we need it. Life is pain eased by the comforts we scratch on the walls. In beauty's service, Keats lied. Truth is a moving target, but beauty we can see, touch, and hold. It can't return because it never left us: we left it. The twentieth century made beauty that's not selling us something hard to share and rare to see, but it's still here, ready whenever we are.

THE ANTI-SOCIALITE:
LIFE WITH AN ASPERGER'S CHILD

Denis Seguin
The Walrus

On the first day of Autism 2006, the Geneva Centre for Autism International Symposium at the Metro Toronto Convention Centre, the main event was a presentation by Tony Attwood. As the audience trickled into the 1,330-seat John Bassett Theatre, the image on the giant screen at stage centre was a tranquil expanse of ocean. A man in a suit crossed the stage to organize something on the lectern. Three women in front of me began murmuring. It was Attwood. Another woman went up to the stage and called to him. Smiling, he moved forward to greet her and then folded himself down to the stage floor, his head resting in one upturned palm as they chatted. The murmur intensified, coming from all directions. "He's even lying down for her," a woman whispered. Another took out her digital camera. "We've got to get our picture with him."

If Asperger's syndrome has a patron saint, it is Tony Attwood. Born and educated in England, he now heads the Macgregor Specialist Centre in Brisbane, Australia; is an adjunct associate professor at Griffith University in Queensland; and is considered one of the world's leading experts on AS. To many, Attwood literally wrote the book: *The Complete Guide to Asperger's Syndrome* encompasses twenty-five-plus years of clinical experience and research. Having worked with more than 2,000 people (of all ages) with AS, he is a mentor to a generation of occupational therapists and a guru for parents.

Once rarely diagnosed and largely misunderstood, autism—of which AS is a subset, a relatively mild form that generally allows those who have it to function—is now thought to be fairly common. In the 1970s, one in 2,500 individuals might have received the diagnosis; today in the US, it applies to approximately one in 150 children, an increase attributable to better awareness and broader diagnosis. Autism has been reconceptualized from something quite specific into a "spectrum disorder," a wide arc encompassing classic low-functioning autism—the person locked in his own world—and conditions that are undetectable to the casual observer. Spotting it is akin to birdwatching: you might have to spend many hours before catching a glimpse of a person's AS tendencies.

In the scheme of autism, a diagnosis of AS is a blessing, but a mixed one, given that we live in such a social world. "Aspy" children, as Attwood calls them, tend to be diagnosed around age seven or eight, just as their socially-oriented, neurotypical peers start to notice their difference. My son was diagnosed with AS when he was eight. Nearly three years later, my wife and I are still learning just how powerful and arbitrary the social world is.

I had spoken with Attwood before the symposium. His accent and elocution are not unlike those of C-3PO, the hyper-correct android of *Star Wars* fame. I told him about my son's concern about AS: specifically, why does it have to be syndrome? To J., Syndrome is the name of the villain in the animated film and video game *The Incredibles*. "Technically, a syndrome describes a pattern that has a detrimental effect on that person's quality of life," said Attwood. "Lots of people feel anxious or sad, but it only becomes a depression clinically when it affects that person's quality of life." Suggesting that "syndrome" is an improvement on "disorder," in his book, Attwood quotes an American child's complaint to his mother: "Actually, I'm not in disorder. I am definitely in order."

Autistic children, in fact, tend to be driven by order. They might line up objects—cars, blocks, dolls—and can be sent into a blind fury if those orderly rows are disturbed. As an autistic or AS person matures, this compulsion for order and systematizing manifests itself in obsessive interests, which often become that person's salvation or damnation. Darius McCollum, a forty-three-year-old New Yorker, has spent a third of his life in prison because of his overwhelming compulsion for all things rail related: in 2005, he pled guilty to grand larceny for attempting to steal a locomotive. He blamed his Asperger's. Richard Borcherds could have entered Cambridge's mathematics department at twelve years old. His childhood obsession was building polyhedrons. At age thirty-eight—the year he won the Fields Medal, the mathematics equivalent of the Nobel Prize—he was diagnosed with AS. He is now a math professor at Berkeley.

My wife and I began "explaining" our son long before he was diagnosed. We had little choice: as a two-year-old at the Montessori daycare in London, England, J. was the only child who ran away from his mother when it was time to go home. "He doesn't seem to like transitions," one of the caregivers told us. "He doesn't seem to like transitions," my wife and I would mutter to each other as we tried to coax him out from under the sofa after he'd been playing at a neighbour's apartment. He would scream and twist as we carried him—like two screws with an escaped convict—back upstairs to our flat. Once home, he would calm down as if nothing had happened.

He seemed a normal child in many ways. He loved bath time, was a giggling cherub watching a rubber dolphin slide down the tub wall.

But there were premonitions of extremes. He absorbed storybooks and could repeat them in their entirety: "The Owl and the Pussycat went to sea in a be-yoo-tee-full peagreen boat . . ." He showed tremendous visual acuity, drawing with originality. He was great with numbers, and had a precocious ability to finish complicated puzzles unassisted. He baffled us.

"He's sensitive," people would say.

"He doesn't do goodbyes."

"A dreamer lost in his thoughts . . . All intelligent kids are like that . . ." We heard it all—words a parent wants to hear.

It wasn't until we moved back to Canada, had a second son and then a third, that we realized our eldest was actually another kind of person. He didn't seem to see other people as people—not even his own brothers. He was interested in them, but impassively, objectively. When one of them was hurt and was being comforted, J. would walk over with a picture book and ask to have something explained, oblivious to both the suffering and the nurturing before him. "Don't you see that your brother is upset?" "Why is he crying?" "You didn't hear him fall from the bed? You were sitting right there." It was another matter altogether if one of his brothers disturbed his equilibrium: an accidental bump in the hallway resulted in extreme reprisal.

In the summer of 2003, my sister-in-law, a fellow journalist, asked if we had ever heard of Asperger's syndrome. We had not, and we were suspicious of it—no doubt another maladie du jour. She had mentioned J. to a friend whose son had been diagnosed. There were similarities, such as lack of eye contact, a sophisticated vocabulary, and a monotone voice that typifies "the little professor syndrome," as AS is also known. But not enough to convince us, or for us to realize that some of J.'s tics were in fact "stimming"—repetitive, self-stimulating behaviour.

It took another year before we sought professional advice. Our family doctor put us in touch with the Centre for Addiction and Mental Health (CAMH) in Toronto. My wife took J. to meet Dr Leon Sloman, head of psychiatry, and returned home with a positive diagnosis—and news that Sloman wanted to meet me.

Sloman's office is much like that of other distinguished academics: books stacked haphazardly or strewn about the floor, an embarrassingly old computer. He was preparing a PowerPoint presentation about AS, and on the screen was a list of responses to a diagnosis. I suggested he add "parental anger." He looked up, his face showing the signs of a career diagnosing people like J. and taking questions from people like me.

But AS only entered the diagnostic nomenclature in 1994, Sloman told me in a later meeting. "I began to get referrals and to make the diagnosis maybe five, six, or seven years ago," he said. "It always takes a few years to percolate. It's exploded over the past few years." Difficult as it is to consider one's child part of an explosion, my initial feeling was relief. In hindsight, I see that relief as a reflexive impulse engendered by our faith in medical science: great, now we can fix him.

While a relatively new addition to the autism lexicon, AS was first identified more than sixty years ago, in the research of two Austrian psychologists working with autistic children in different parts of the world. It happened almost simultaneously: first, when Vienna clinician Hans Asperger coined the term "autistic psychopathy," and then through the work of Leo Kanner, who had fled Nazi Germany for the academic sanctuary of Johns Hopkins in Baltimore. Asperger wrote his pioneering paper in 1944, but "Die 'autistischen Psychopathen' im Kindesalter" ("Autistic psychopathy in children") didn't gain broad currency until 1991, when it was translated into English by Uta Frith, a psychologist at the University of London's cognitive development unit. "One can spot such children instantly," Asperger wrote. "They are recognizable from small details, for instance, the way they enter the consulting room at their first visit, their behaviour in the first few moments and the first words they utter."

Reading Asperger's case studies provides parents of an Aspy child with a distant mirror. "Normal children acquire the necessary social habits without being consciously aware of them, they learn instinctively. [Autistic children] have to learn everything via the intellect," Asperger surmised in a resonant description that has been picked up by contemporary clinicians. In his acclaimed book *The Explosive Child*, Ross W. Greene analyzes an everyday encounter in the schoolyard. A boy approaches another boy, smiles, slaps him on the back, and says, "How's it goin'?" An autistic or AS brain might interpret the situation as follows: What does the smile mean? How hard was the slap? Has this same boy done this before? How hard was the slap compared to earlier slaps? Does he slap other boys? And that's the first step; the Aspy child's own mental and physical response has yet to be formulated.

In the mid-1980s, Frith, working with Simon Baron-Cohen, then her PhD student, and another scientist, Alan Leslie, developed an analysis called "theory of mind." It refers to the ability to put yourself in someone else's shoes, a skill, writes Frith, that "enables us to predict other people's behaviour. Thinking about what others think, rather than what is going on in the physical world outside, is essential for engaging in complex social activity, because it underpins our ability to cooperate and to learn from each other." In autistic individuals, theory of mind is either disabled or entirely absent, which makes them very frustrating companions. Neurotypical people, programmed for social interaction, tend to dismiss those with autism or AS as anti-social. But to say people with AS have difficulty socializing makes it sound as if they don't care for cocktail parties. Similarly, when AS children attempt to interact with their peers, failure and rejection can amplify low self-esteem. They give up trying, because it only makes them feel worse.

Aspy children are not always happily adrift in their own little bubbles; like most everyone else, they yearn for kinship. Unfortunately, it tends to be on their terms.

The social world is intuitive, and its conventions so ingrained in collective behaviour that we barely notice them. Humans are profoundly social, and when an individual fails to fit in, others—no matter how modern, savvy, kind-hearted or well intentioned, empathic or sainted—tend to react negatively. We are hardwired to identify and isolate aberrant behaviour, any signs that run contrary to the group. Knowing this, parenting Aspy children can be a minefield. At what point in a developing relationship—with a new neighbour, the parent of a potential friend, a soccer coach—do we explain J.? The first meltdown? The second unbridled criticism of a teammate's failings? Should we have to explain at all?

For a parent of an autism spectrum child, anger is never far from the surface. On day three of the symposium, I sat in on a lunchtime session cheerily titled Dads 'R' Us: A Session by Fathers for Fathers. Two of the three men were fathers of children with classic autism. One of them paced with barely contained agony, seething as he described his diminished hopes for his child and his own thwarted career ambitions. I recognized that rage, the crushing letdown that comes with the realization that there is no easy fix, no long-term cure. The recognition came with a shaming relief: our situation is nowhere near as extreme. But here, too, lies a problem. There's a tendency to say, "It's not that bad," to brush aside the experiences of those who have gone before us, and let our son muddle through. And then I just get mad at myself. My son needs my help. He needs advocates—at school, in the park, even at home.

More so than in cases of classic autism, the figurative expression "stumbling block" provides insight into the AS individual's world view. Aspy children tend to interpret every utterance literally. "What block? I don't see one. And I'm not stumbling. I'm walking normally." Neurotypical children intuitively skip over superficial social exchanges and don't ask, as Aspy children do, "Why would you ask me, 'How are you doing?' when you can plainly see that I am fine?" Not until you've taken an existential step sideways from the social world do you appreciate the utility of such interaction as a lubricant to making your way. As Aspy children decode their environment—interpreting everything literally—to the unaware observer, they may appear closed off or unwilling to acknowledge others.

For J., the social world can be an upsetting, even dangerous place. An example: the morning walk to school is the usual collection of neighbouring parents and children. My son walks ahead of them. Another group of parents with small children is ahead of him. My son walks through the small children as you or I might walk through a cornfield. Not over them, but brushing past them. It's a bombardment of signals to the parents of these children—this boy is different; he is not to be trusted near small children; he is to be avoided.

Onstage, Attwood is ideally suited to his audience, mostly professionals who deal with people on the autism spectrum, parents, and a few AS individuals. The information is dense but structured, the delivery spiced with pathos and humour, with mime and performance acts such as Spot the Aspy. For this routine, Attwood apes the carriage, ambulation, and focus of an adult AS male—back rigid but tilted slightly forward, arms and legs straight, laserlike eyes gazing at a point on the ground two metres in front of him. The laughter is rich with recognition. But it is Attwood's gift for metaphor that makes his presentation so lucid and welcoming.

"Imagine a clearing in a forest," he says. "That clearing represents brain development. In [it], a number of tree saplings are growing. In the typical child, one tree grows quickly and dominates the clearing, shades the other plants, takes all the nutrients from the soil, and inhibits the development of competing plants. Now, for the typical child that [tree] is the social part of the brain. But if that plant is not as dominant and doesn't inhibit the others, then other plants will thrive. Your brain inhibits other experiences, especially the sensory experiences. This means that these guys may have an ability that we have inhibited, in hearing, smell, touch, taste." In other words, people on the autism spectrum may be socially awkward, but they are uniquely aware and sensitive to perceptions neurotypical individuals simply miss.

Attwood calls the positive attributes associated with autism the Three Ms: mechanical, mathematical, and musical ability—Dustin Hoffman's character in *Rain Man*, or Geoffrey Rush's pianist in *Shine*. But because AS is at the milder end of the spectrum, an AS person with one of these "islets of ability" is more likely to find a traditional place in society. Indeed, there is strong evidence that AS adults are over-represented in the ranks of engineering and information technology. Incidences of autism diagnosis are greater in regions associated with the high-tech industry, such as California's Silicon Valley and Redmond, Washington, home of Microsoft. One explanation for these regional spikes is assortative mating: geeks mating with geeks. In a groundbreaking 2001 article, "The Geek Syndrome," published in the technology magazine *Wired*, Steve Silberman wrote, "As more women enter the IT workplace, guys who might never have had a prayer of finding a kindred spirit suddenly discover that she's hacking Perl scripts in the next cubicle."

Research points strongly to a genetic link. Simon Baron-Cohen, Uta Frith's protege, now a professor of developmental psychopathology at the University of Cambridge and director of its Autism Research Centre, is a leader in the field. In *The Essential Difference: The Truth about the Male and Female Brain*, Baron-Cohen points to autism in twins. If an identical twin has autism, the chances of the other twin having an autism spectrum disorder are between 60 and 90 percent, whereas the coincidence in fraternal twins is about 20 percent. Since identicals share 100 percent of their genes, while fraternals share about 50 percent, "this strongly suggests that autism is heritable," argues Baron-Cohen. People diagnosed with AS tend to have a parent or grandparent with similar traits—one of the reasons Sloman wanted to see me: Aspy kids often have (undiagnosed) Aspy dads.

Baron-Cohen postulates what he calls the "extreme male brain." Using an extensive range of self-directed surveys, he charted a graph of humans on two axes: empathizing and systematizing. Neurotypical females figure slightly higher on the empathy axis, with men farther along the systematizing axis. But autistic males and females both show significantly higher rates of systematizing, and are lower on the empathy scale, indicating that autism spectrum individuals of both sexes tend to have brains dominated by male systematizing impulses.

I suggested to Baron-Cohen that AS is a condition we should try to harness, not cure. He concurred and, in an article published in the millennium edition of the journal *Development and Psychopathlogy*, wrote: "I wanted to shift people away from the idea that autism spectrum is a simple medical disease, which was the prevailing view and in some quarters still is. Disorder is an inappropriate term. AS involves a different form of neurological wiring in the way the person thinks differently and perceives differently. But that doesn't necessarily mean that they are worse than other people."

In her introductory essay, "Asperger and His Syndrome," published seventeen years ago in the collection *Autism and Asperger Syndrome*,

Frith wrote, "Asperger pleaded for the recognition of such children, pointing out the potential that they had to offer society . . . he also suggested parallels between autism, scientific originality and inversion." The Roman poet Seneca, Frith reminds us, observed that there is no genius without madness, a notion (with us at least since Aristotle linked melancholia and creativity) that is now being seriously considered with regards to autism generally, and AS specifically. Says Baron-Cohen, "Of course, in certain situations—like when you're required to socialize—it is a disability. But in other contexts, AS may confer certain strengths, and you wouldn't want to treat those, or reduce or eradicate those qualities."

In keeping with the view that autism is linked to genius, Michael Fitzgerald, a psychiatry professor at Trinity College Dublin, has analyzed biographies of artists and philosophers to conduct a kind of posthumous diagnosis of high-functioning notables with, potentially at least, autism or AS. The lineup is a cultural dream team: Mozart, Swift, Van Gogh, Bartók, Orwell, Warhol, Gould, etc.

Could J. be a genius trapped inside an eleven-year-old with the frustration threshold of a toddler? Maybe, but for every potential Glenn Gould wandering Toronto, there are many Aspys living on disability because they can't hold down a job. My wife and I have met them: adults who come in to CAMH to talk about life and what our children can expect. Stocking shelves at a drugstore, working in the mailroom—these are considered success stories. Where will my son be in ten years?

My lineage is all about "eccentric normality," the term used by Lorna Wing, another contributor to *Autism and Asperger Syndrome*, to describe the condition. My wife and I play the game of looking at relatives for clues. We accentuate the positive, but still, a good number of my kin might be described as functioning oddballs and on the introverted side of the social divide. Maybe J. is a part of this, and as such maybe he's okay. After all, he's in regular classes at school in French immersion; doesn't run away (too much); doesn't disrupt the class (too much); he "presents" reasonably well—a seemingly shallow concern, until you've experienced an AS child who doesn't present well.

Every Wednesday at CAMH, J. attends a social skills group organized by the Aspergers Society of Ontario and guided by a team of occupational therapists and speech pathologists. The parents have their own group discussion led by autism spectrum specialists. At the end of each session, one of the occupational therapists comes into the parents' meeting and discusses what the kids are working on. "Today we talked about good fidgeting. For example, jangling change in your pants pockets is good fidgeting. Picking up a chair and rocking it back and forth on your head is bad fidgeting."

Which is why we as parents are at pains to explain that AS is a communication disorder, not a behavioural one. There is nothing wrong, per se, with rocking a chair on your head. It is what other people make of such actions, and negative (though neurotypical) interpretations of these behaviours often lead to problems. Let's add Sartre to the Aspy pantheon: "Hell is other people."

One of the speakers at the symposium, Ros Blackburn—a more classically autistic person, with an astonishing capacity for public presentation but not individual interaction—described a trip to a play with a group of mentally disabled people. While others enjoyed the play, she sat through it without processing any of it as theatre. She had been transfixed by the physical minutiae, like a feather from a costume alighting on the stage floor.

Blackburn told us of her great desire to go to McDonald's. This brought surprised laughter from the audience. Surely a jest. But Blackburn doesn't jest—she's incapable of it. She only speaks the truth, a truth disarming in its poignant bluntness. Later, I approached her; there was mutual trepidation. She could not look at me. And I felt awkward trying not to search for her gaze. I asked her to explain why she cannot walk into a McDonald's.

"It's the whole working out of what's going on," she said, staring past my elbow, "of making sense of the environment. Knowing, for example, that you have to move forward as the line progresses. I know I have to wait in a queue, but I have to wait here." She started to move her feet. "Then, in a few seconds' time, you have to wait not here but there. And that becomes the 'here.' And knowing that somebody [behind the counter] looking up and saying 'Next' means I have to move up. Because she hasn't said, 'Ros, which burger would you like?' They're just looking up. And that means I've got to place my order. They might say, 'Would you like a bag?' and I have to work out does she mean do I like their bags? Or do I want to use a bag? And on it goes."

On it goes. A friend and her three daughters came to stay at the cottage for a week. I was serving dessert, and J., then ten, stood expectantly. I gave a bowl to one girl, then J. reached to take one. "Guests first," I said, passing him over to give another girl a bowl. "Why? Why?" The anger flooded his face. "I was next in line." He had his serving within twenty seconds, but ten minutes later was still fuming over the injustice of the concept that guests should be served first. It was a boneheaded move on my part. A simple comment to prepare him and adjust his expectations would have spared him the fury and shame of losing control in front of guests. What was I thinking?

J. still baffles us; maybe he always will. Three years after the diagnosis, my wife and I are now working with a psychologist, learning to think like J. thinks, learning to think like an Aspy. The idea is to predict and thus avoid incidents rather than deal with the aftermath. Objectively, it's highly instructive—you interpret the world differently. Subjectively, it's exhausting. But that exhaustion gives us an inkling of the challenge J. and his Aspy peers face every moment they spend with other people. The long-term goal is to raise his frustration threshold, to learn to resolve his inner turmoil.

In the 1960s, according to Frith, "the general view was that autism is an emotional disorder with a psychological basis, and the burden of blame was put on the mother. This was terribly wrong." The fact of autism forced scientists to reconsider accepted wisdom about brain development, "not as a big bowl of spaghetti tangles, but more like a building with different floors and rooms." Attwood likens the diagnostic process to a hundred-piece jigsaw puzzle. "Each piece is a fragment or characteristic of AS. Eighty or more pieces, and you're there . . . There are certain essential corner or edge pieces you need." But, he adds, "everyone has ten to fifteen pieces. So the question is not 'Have you got any?' but rather 'How many have you got?'"

THE BIG DECISION

Chris Turner
Alberta Views

The first time I heard tell of a notion of a nuclear power plant in northern Alberta, it was the punchline to an anecdote, intended as a wry slice of gallows humour. It was in the spring of 2006, and I was at an intimate conference in Germany concerned with the converging calamities of peak oil and climate change. The seminar table was crowded with oil field geologists, green power experts and environmental campaigners, the talk portentous and often heated. These were enormous issues, the kind that defined eras and ushered in new epochs, and if few in the room agreed on the exact steps needed to be taken to avoid catastrophe, everyone knew that steps had to be taken, and that they were giant steps indeed.

At the coffee break, I fell into conversation with my neighbour, an energy reporter for *The Economist*. He learned I was from Calgary, and launched into a story about a research trip he'd made to the city a couple years previously, just as the oil sands boom's rumblings were growing loud enough to be heard even in the London offices of his employer. He'd been bemused, he explained, by Calgary's new-found self-importance. There'd been, in particular, a round-table discussion involving a handful of top oil patch executives and government bigwigs, and my *Economist* colleague, aiming to provoke, had asked about a boast he'd heard—that Alberta could one day top Saudi Arabia in oil production. Wouldn't that, he wondered, require ramping up production by a factor of 10? Where would the province find the energy to fuel a mining operation of that scale?

The round-table participants refused to dismiss the notion out of hand, instead tossing out blue-sky suggestions. If the price of a barrel of oil were high enough, there were simply no known limits to what could be done. One of them even offhandedly suggested you could build a bunch of nuclear power plants in the oil patch to provide as much juice as it took.

The Economist's energy reporter[1] thought that was hilarious. Here, for the record, is *The Economist* itself, in 1998, on the subject of nuclear

---

[1] I will preserve my colleague's anonymity, both because the conference itself was intended as an educational exercise for working journalists and was thus semi-officially off the record, and because I later heard this same *Economist* reporter argue at length with the editor of the European edition of *Time* that the absence of bylines in *The Economist* was absolutely critical to its reputation and moral authority.

power plants: "not one, anywhere in the world, makes commercial sense."

So imagine my surprise, barely a year after that German conference, to find this headline above the fold on the front page of the *Calgary Herald*: "Alberta nuclear future a step closer." Now how, exactly, had it so quickly come to this? In what fevered moment had round-table brainstorming been transformed into a formal application to the Canadian Nuclear Safety Commission? And, moreover, why? Was this boomtown madness, naked greed, or grim necessity? A white elephant soon to be born, or a phoenix set to rise from the carbon-choked flames of our fossil-fuel bonfire? Salvation or a new face of doom?

If this was ever a joke, it isn't one any longer. These are profound questions, and they cut to the core of the kind of province Alberta has become and the kind of future it wants to build for itself. The very basis of the global energy economy has just begun a fundamental shift, and the long-term success of any given society—and possibly of humanity itself— very likely rests on how wisely it steers this new course. No viable option should be dismissed out of hand, but neither should any proposal—least of all a development project with a ten-year construction phase, a sixty-year lifespan, a waste product with a half-life of 24,100 years and a price tag in the billions—be taken at face value, nor pursued until it has undergone the most thorough and rigorous evaluation possible.

That kind of due diligence is well beyond my ability and expertise. I've attempted instead simply to outline the facts of the case and properly frame the criteria for such an analysis. Should Alberta exercise its nuclear option? I can't offer a definitive answer. I'm not sure, though, if I would want to live much longer in a place that saw it as the only option for its energy future. Because a society with a focus that narrow probably won't have much of a future.

At the end of August 2007, a fledgling company called Energy Alberta Corp. filed an application with the Canadian Nuclear Safety Commission to build a nuclear power plant in the Peace Country. Energy Alberta was founded a couple of years earlier by Hank Swartout and Wayne Henuset, two oil patch veterans. The initial motivation came in 2004, when a hurricane destroyed a house Henuset had built in Florida—which awakened him, he later told the *National Post*, to the realities of climate change. Henuset got to talking to a physicist about the "cleaner, safer, more reliable, dependable and stable" nature of nuclear power— so went Henuset's recollection—and a seed was planted.

Details of the Energy Alberta plan emerged throughout the fall of 2007: the proposed facility would consist of two reactors generating

2,200 megawatts of power, 70 percent of it intended for a single unnamed private customer whose identity never emerged. At subsequent press conferences, the company claimed their electricity would be used to fuel rapidly expanding oil sands operations, but several major oil companies soon stated they had no such needs—indeed the Athabasca oil sands region is, at present, a net electricity exporter, and most of the large players there have already invested in other sources to provide for their power needs through 2020. Energy Alberta then switched its focus to the provincial power grid, citing reports that suggested the province may need 4,000 megawatts or more of additional generating capacity by 2016.

In March 2008, Bruce Power—a public/private partnership based in Ontario, where it is the province's largest independent power generator, operating six nuclear reactors—bought Energy Alberta and rechristened it Bruce Power Alberta. Soon after, this newly formed subsidiary announced it would be seeking approval for a "$10-billion-plus nuclear complex," a cluster of four reactors with a total generating capacity of over 4,000 megawatts. In April, the Alberta government established a four-person review panel to study the viability of nuclear power for the province. One member of the panel is John Luxat, the former president of the Canadian Nuclear Society, a sister body to a major nuclear-industry lobby group. Bruce Power Alberta's chief lobbyist, meanwhile, is Randy Dawson, who served as the provincial Tories' campaign manager in this year's election. In early July, a study commissioned by Bruce Power Alberta was released, claiming that the Peace Country nuclear plant would create 2,700 jobs and generate $12-billion in revenues over the ten years of its construction.

Press reports on the Bruce Power Alberta proposal's specifics have been accompanied by much rumour and speculation. The company's Ontario parent turned out to be in talks with the Saskatchewan government as well, fuelling fears of a prairie showdown over who would win the $12-billion prize. And other nuclear energy companies—most notably the French giant Areva—joined the fray, with executives jetting into Calgary for closed-door meetings followed by brief statements in which it was asserted that the Bruce proposal was nowhere near large enough to meet Alberta's energy needs by itself. Meanwhile, up in the Peace Country, a sizeable, strident, and well-organized opposition to the nuclear plant quickly emerged. Bruce Power Alberta, for its part, set up a storefront office in Peace River.

The nuclear drama now unfolding in the Peace Country is a small, self-contained version of a much broader conversation, a reenactment at rural Alberta scale of the global nuclear debate in the age of climate change. In the wake of the industry's infamous disasters of the 1970s and 1980s—first the barely avoided catastrophe at Three Mile Island in the United States in 1979, then the real deal in Chernobyl in 1986—nuclear power had all but disappeared from the modern energy game. After the Darlington nuclear plant in southern Ontario was finally completed in 1993—well past deadline, at seven times its expected cost by some estimates—Canadians, too, lost interest in nukes. Nuclear energy had famously been touted as a modern-age miracle bringing near-limitless power "too cheap to meter." But after a half-century of mammoth subsidies and well-funded research, the industry hadn't even managed to bring global nuclear generation capacity to the same level as burning wood, at a premium nobody was any longer willing to pay—particularly since it continued to churn out radioactive waste for which nobody had developed a permanent disposal solution.

In recent years, however, global awareness of the high price and increasing scarcity of oil and gas and the catastrophic consequences of continuing to burn it (and especially its cousin coal) at current rates has rapidly moved from the fringe to the mainstream, and nuclear power has reinvented itself in response. The transformation has been breathtaking in its speed and thoroughness. Heretofore all but synonymous with the idea of hazardous waste, the nuclear industry has become the realistic green alternative—green because its plants belch no greenhouse gases to pump their juice[2] and realistic because, well, what other emissions-free choice is there that produces energy in 1,000-megawatt increments?

Support for this argument, which now adorns the homepage of every self-respecting nuclear energy company's website, has emerged from some unexpected quarters. The prominent environmental scientist James Lovelock, for example, best-known as the progenitor of the "Gaia hypothesis," has become a vocal supporter of nuclear power, which he believes is the only fuel source that might be capable of avoiding the ecological Armageddon he foresees as imminent. And Stewart Brand, the erstwhile founder of the Whole Earth Catalog, has also become a nuclear advocate, arguing that only nuclear power can meet the outsized needs of the modern world without generating catastrophic levels of emissions. This line of reasoning was succinctly summarized in a recent *Wired* cover story: "There's no question that nuclear power is the most climate-friendly industrial-scale energy source . . . [T]he reality is that

---

[2] This ignores the argument that uranium mining generates significant amounts of greenhouse gas emissions and leaves tailing ponds laden with heavy metals in its wake.

every serious effort at carbon accounting reaches the same conclusion: nukes win. Only wind comes close—and that's when it's blowing."

It was in the pages of *GQ*, of all places, that I came across probably the most persuasive argument I've yet found in favour of the nuclear option. This was a feature story by Wil S. Hylton, a self-professed "environmentalist." Hylton's essay was a particularly passionate lament in the lesser-of-two-evils vein, building upon a detailed analysis of the impact of the Three Mile Island disaster—which, he notes, had a body count of zero. The toxic stew spewed by coal-fired power generation, on the other hand, routinely kills thousands of people each year—even before climate change is included in its deadly cost. But still, much of the world continues to oppose nuclear power, which obliges us to burn yet more coal.

Hylton: "What drives this opposition, in many cases, is the conflation of magnitude with probability. That is, when people worry about nuclear power, what they worry about is the scale of an accident, not the likelihood. In this regard, nuclear power is just the opposite of the nation's coal-fired plants, where harm to the environment is both ruinous and certain but comfortingly slow. It may take decades or even centuries for the effects of particle soot, acid rain and global warming to claim a million lives. By contrast, the nightmare scenario with nuclear power is decades of cheap, plentiful, pollution-free energy—followed by a sudden meltdown that wipes out a city."

I found myself nodding along. If our only choice is between nuclear and coal, then it was no contest at all. I was all but persuaded. It was only on further rumination, though, that it occurred to me that Hylton's argument—any argument I've heard in favour of nuclear power—rested on a few pervasive but mostly baseless myths. That nuclear power is both cheap and plentiful, to name two. (And never mind the pollution-free part; nukes undoubtedly produce far fewer emissions per kilowatt hour than fossil fuels, and the essential truth of this is why it's become the cornerstone of the industry's rebranding campaign.)

The most egregious myth, however—the one that could damn Alberta to a nuclear future as the twenty-first-century economy races greenly past—is the one that says it's our only choice. Allow me to be exceedingly blunt: that's just bullshit.

Before we get to the cow pies, let's take a quick look at the rest of the myths of the nuclear renaissance. The Peace Country's microcosmic version of the conversation lays out most of this. To wit: that Alberta, even more than the world in general, is a rapidly expanding economy with a growing and ever-more-power-hungry population base, making the addition of many thousands of megawatts of electricity a near-future necessity; that only nuclear plants can supply this power in a cost-effective and timely manner; and that it will produce no greenhouse gases and create thousands of jobs to boot.

The job-creation angle is as unassailable as the emissions claim: a $10-billion-plus infrastructure project employs lots of people, and big power plants need lots of long-term staff. The cost effectiveness of nuclear power, however, is a more dubious assertion. Benchmarking power prices is a particularly disingenuous kind of fool's game—there is not a truly rational energy market in any jurisdiction on earth—but even by the current, tilted standards, nuclear power and its fifty years of subsidies and taxpayer-funded cost overruns comes to market at a price, per kilowatt hour, about equal to wind power. It's worth further noting that wind energy, which was virtually nonexistent as a commercial power source when Three Mile Island had its flirtation with meltdown, already competes on purely economic terms with any other energy source everywhere it's been expanded to industrial scale—Alberta included.

What's more, not one of the current generation of nuclear plants—which includes the CANDU reactors that Bruce Power Alberta proposes to build in the Peace Country—has been built on time and on budget outside of autocratic, environmental-regulation-free regimes such as China. The speed-of-deployment argument is even more specious, given that even the best-case scenario put forward by Bruce Power Alberta itself would have the first fission-generated kilowatt hour hitting Alberta's grid at least nine years from today. That's another decade in the most volatile energy market of the industrial era; bear in mind that if you rewind nine years (the first half-dozen of which were relatively stable), a barrel of oil was running you less than the cost of a steak at Earls. And so understand that anyone's estimate of the relative costs of fuel sources—including uranium—in 2017 is barely better than a wild guess.

The same goes for estimates of future fuel consumption, which is where the argument for the necessity of nuclear energy (in Alberta or anywhere else) begins to unravel. At current consumption rates, Alberta will need 4,000 more megawatts of power by 2016, but I know of no credible energy expert who would claim that current consumption rates will be sustainable over the sixty-year life of a nuclear plant. Indeed, for reasons of both fuel scarcity and emissions-reduction necessity, the International Energy Agency projects that fuel conservation will be the single largest change in the global energy picture by mid-century. "The cheapest form of new energy is to use a lot less"—says Dave Hughes, recently retired energy resource analyst from the Geological Survey of Canada.

I first met Hughes at the Gaining Ground sustainability conference in Calgary in May 2008, where he gave what he said was his 147th presentation over the past six years outlining the real crux of the global energy crisis. To wit: that no one existing fuel source can possibly make up the inevitable energy deficit that the status quo will create by mid-century. Oil is at or near its global production peak and gas will follow, likely by mid-century at the latest. The nuclear industry, he explained, would have to embark on its biggest building boom ever just to replace outdated plants and meet modest growth forecasts which would see nuclear grow in real terms but decline in market share over the next couple of decades. "Nuclear could be part of the solution," Hughes told me. "In the longer term, though, I really don't think, you know, given that fossil fuels are 89 percent of our energy consumption, that business as usual as we enjoy it today is really possible for more than maybe a decade or two. So I think it behooves us to rethink the way we consume energy."

This, ultimately, is the most glaring and potentially catastrophic absence in Alberta's nuclear debate: the question of what kind of place the Alberta of 2017 (or 2057) wants to be, starting with the energy it will use to fuel that future. Because—to dispose, finally, of the biggest cow pie—there is in fact another choice. For some reason, though, it's easy to miss. Consider the point in Wil Hylton's otherwise convincing pro-nuke argument in *GQ* when he lost all credibility. He was explaining how eliminating nuclear plants from the US electricity grid would require increasing production from other sources by 25 percent. Hylton: "Since that's not possible for most current renewables—like wind, solar and hydroelectric farms, which are already maxed out—the real cost of eliminating today's nuclear power supply would be an immediate 30 percent increase in the nation's coal, gas and oil plants." Spot the cow pie: "most current renewables . . . are already maxed out." I don't know what planet this assertion blipped in from, but it's the same one on which only nuclear power can scale up to meet projected demand, and it's not the one you and I live on.

Here are some underpublicized facts about the planet we do live on. According to a report by BC Hydro, which is already well integrated with Alberta's grid, there is more than 2,000 megawatts of readily accessible, cost-effective run-of-river hydroelectric power available in British Columbia at present. (As far as I know, no such study has been conducted of Alberta's own water-power resources.) In Germany, which crowds almost thirty times the population of Alberta into a little over half the land mass, room has been found just in the last ten years for more than 20,000 megawatts of wind energy—more than double Alberta's current power-generating capacity from all sources. Plans are now in the works to erect 17,000 megawatts' worth of wind turbines in the windy barrens of west Texas, which bear such geographic similarity to southeastern Alberta that the latter sometimes appear as the former in movies. One Texas company, BroadStar Wind Systems, has just announced the birth of the era of ubiquitous dollar-per-watt wind generation, and I won't bore you with the econometric details except to say that this is far cheaper than anything the nuclear industry even pretends to be capable of delivering.

Of course, anyone who's driven past the windswept buttes west of Fort Macleod lately knows that Alberta has already demonstrated its suitability for industrial-scale wind power. The province's installed wind-energy capacity has expanded from zero to about 525 megawatts in less than a decade with no real encouragement from the provincial government, and Alberta led the nation in wind power until Ontario's ambitious Standard Offer program gave its wind industry the kickstart that has thus far been absent here. In the ten years since the first wind farm was erected in Pincher Creek, Alberta, the cost per kilowatt-hour has steadily declined (notwithstanding a brief recent increase owing to excessive demand for new turbines worldwide). In an era of carbon taxes and caps, wind power's long-term comparative cost advantage is pretty much assured—especially since, unlike nuclear or fossil fuels, a wind turbine's fuel source is free of charge and unaffected by the volatile global markets currently wreaking havoc on conventional energy prices.

In Taiwan and China, and especially Germany and California, meanwhile, solar companies of various stripes are constructing gigawatt-capacity solar-panel production lines. These are factories, to be constructed in less than a year, capable of fabricating enough solar panels every year to add a gigawatt of electricity to the grid of any customer who comes calling. A gigawatt is 1,000 megawatts, so any given one of these new factories could add 7,000 megawatts of solar energy to their respective grids by the time Bruce Power Alberta's 4,000-megawatt plant is complete, and all of these production facilities are projected to create a great many jobs and cost significantly less than $10-billion-plus to construct.

I want to belabour this last point: several of these gigawatt-scale solar-panel factories will primarily serve the German market, which has a solar resource about as abundant as southern Alaska's. This is simply because Germany has decided to prepare itself now for the radically altered energy economy of the twenty-first century and beyond. In the short term, this has produced some less-than-ideal solutions—buying nuclear-generated electricity from France, for example, and giving serious consideration to commissioning new coal plants—but these measures are being undertaken in the context of a fundamental shift in the nation's energy regime.[3]

I was in eastern Germany not too long ago, touring the first 500-megawatt production line being built by Nanosolar, one of the companies that plans to have a gigawatt-capacity factory up and running by 2010. My tour guide was Erik Oldekop, the executive director of its German operations. He saw compelling parallels between the transformative power of renewable energy and digital communications—in particular, the way both technologies favour radically decentralized systems, and the way they liberate small organizations, and even individuals, to participate as producers as well as consumers. "Isn't the electricity company that actually uses central power plants, isn't that the mainframe?" he suggested. "We have very small, very small power plants, one- to ten-megawatt. Isn't that the PC?"

So let's have a discussion, by all means, about Alberta's energy future and the place of nuclear power in it. But let's have it within the proper parameters. Climate change and the end of the age of cheap, abundant fossil fuels oblige Alberta to reconstruct its power grid in a fundamentally different landscape from the one in which it was first built. We know—it is being demonstrated daily—that the economies that will lead the world by mid-century will be powered by the PC of renewables. Do we really need a nuclear mainframe to get us there? Are we really so lacking in foresight? In courage? Why not lead?

---

[3] Germany will draw at least thirty percent of its power from renewable sources by 2030, and it is already a global leader in the production of solar panels and wind turbines; the renewable energy industry currently employs nearly a quarter of a million Germans.

WE CAN NO LONGER BE SACRIFICED

Lori Theresa Waller
Briarpatch

Fort Chipewyan, a tiny northern Alberta hamlet perched on the shores of Lake Athabasca, is historically notable as the location of the province's oldest European settlement, a trading post opened by the Hudson's Bay Company in 1788.

Mention Fort Chipewyan today, though, and what's likely to come to mind for most Albertans is not the eighteenth-century fur trade, but cancer.

The community's residents, mostly indigenous Cree, Dene (Chipewyan), and Métis, are dying in alarming numbers from a variety of cancers and auto-immune disorders, such as lupus and Graves' disease. The situation was first exposed in 2006 when the town's doctor, John O'Connor, went public with his findings that in this small community of 1,000, he had diagnosed at least three cases of a rare bile duct cancer that normally afflicts only one out of 100,000 Canadians.

Before going to the media, O'Connor had been trying for two years to convince the provincial authorities that something was very wrong in Fort Chipewyan. To this day, the province has taken little action, dismissing O'Connor's concerns with a brief statistical report that found the rate of cancer in the hamlet, although 30 percent higher than the rate for Alberta as a whole, was not statistically significant enough to be considered "elevated." The report was heavily criticized by academics, such as ecologist Kevin P. Timoney, for its questionable statistical methodology and lack of peer review.

Many suspect that Fort Chipewyan's health problems have something to do with the fact that it sits less than 200 kilometres downriver from the biggest industrial project on Earth—the wringing of oil from Alberta's tar sands. It's an endeavour that threatens to devastate not only the people of Fort Chipewyan, but dozens of indigenous communities throughout northern Alberta—and perhaps Canada's entire Northwest.

In the area around Fort McMurray, a five-hour drive north of Edmonton, oil companies are ripping up tens of thousands of hectares of boreal forest to get at the region's tar sands deposits. These deposits are estimated to hold about 174 billion barrels of recoverable oil—a staggering 97 percent of Canada's total oil reserves.

Current operations in the region are extracting about 1.2 million barrels of oil a day, a mammoth undertaking that requires digging open-pit mines 100 feet deep and draining large quantities of fresh water from the Athabasca River to boil bitumen, a thick form of petroleum, out of the sand. The bitumen is then converted to a synthetic crude oil in special heavy-oil upgraders, sullying the air with nitrogen oxides, sulphur dioxide, volatile organic compounds, and other known carcinogens.

Waste water and toxic tailings from the mines are pumped into massive reservoirs that collectively cover more than fifty square kilometres. Flanking the river—a mere 150 feet from the bank in some places—these "tailings ponds" contain a toxic brew of naphthenic acid, trace metals, and other pollutants. The ponds are so highly toxic that birds die upon landing on the water—as nearly 500 ducks did this April, when sonar devices intended to scare away birds failed at the Syncrude site.

There have been several leaks of oil and tailings into the river since the 1960s, when Suncor began excavating the first mine. This company admitted in 1997 that its tailings pond was then leaking approximately 1,600 cubic metres of toxic fluid a day into the Athabasca River, the largest freshwater delta in the world. According to Canada's National Energy Board, tailings ponds are linked to "the migration of pollutants through the groundwater system and the risk of leaks to the surrounding soil and surface water . . . The scale of the problem is daunting and current production trends indicate that the volume of fine tailings ponds produced by Suncor and Syncrude alone will exceed one billion cubic metres by the year 2020."

The damage already caused by tar sands pollution "could actually be worse, in some respects, than the Exxon Valdez," says Jeffrey W. Short, a researcher with the Alaska Fisheries Science Center who has studied the infamous 1989 spill, which dumped 11 million gallons of oil off the Alaska coast. As Dr Short explained to journalists in November 2007, contaminants leaking from the tailings ponds can travel quite quickly throughout the oil-soaked sand that forms the river's banks, making contamination of the river water highly likely.

The impact of this seepage on the region's ecosystems is predictable, and quite visible to those who know the environment most intimately. Fort Chipewyan's indigenous people, who rely heavily on fish as part of their diet, have been noticing decreasing fish populations for several years. They report that the fish they do catch are often deformed, covered with lesions and tumors, or have bizarre mutations. Their flesh, sometimes so soft that you can poke your finger through it, is said to smell like burning plastic when it's fried in a pan.

A study recently commissioned by the region's health authority puts chemical names and numbers to the contamination of the Athabasca

River. Drawing water and sediment samples from Lake Athabasca, into which the river of the same name drains, researcher Kevin P. Timoney found elevated levels of several known toxins and carcinogens. Arsenic, mercury, and several polycyclic aromatic hydrocarbons were all present in levels "sufficiently high to present a risk to either humans or wildlife." The report warned that a pregnant woman eating walleye from the lake would consume, on average, twenty-two times the maximum amount of mercury recommended by the World Health Organization.

While all residents in the region of tar sands mines are exposed to health risks from the massive industrial development, it is the indigenous people of the area whose health is most at risk due to their traditional reliance on fish, moose, cattail, and other "country" foods. Many of the toxins and carcinogens released in the mining process are known to bio-accumulate, or become increasingly concentrated in the flesh of animals as they travel up the food chain. The people of Fort Chipewyan are particularly vulnerable because pollutants travelling down the Athabasca River tend to settle in the fine sediment of Lake Athabasca, where they hunt and fish.

Leaders of Fort Chipewyan's two First Nations, the Mikisew Cree and Athabasca Chipewyan, have recently joined fifty-five organizations across Alberta in calling for an immediate moratorium on any approvals for new tar sands extraction projects. At a rally held in August 2007, Chief Roxanne Marcel of the Mikisew Cree First Nation said: "Our message to both levels of government, to Albertans, to Canadians, and to the world, who may depend on oil sands for their energy solutions, is that we can no longer be sacrificed."

Sacrifice is an apt term. For these indigenous communities, hunting and eating wild fish and game represents a significant source of nutritional sustenance and a core element of their spiritual and cultural identity. By destroying the region's fragile ecology, uncontrolled industrial expansion endangers both the bodies and the cultures of indigenous people.

This is, of course, a sacrifice Canadian governments and companies have been all too willing to make, time and time again, throughout the history of this country. The story of indigenous cultures being destroyed, and of indigenous people bearing the brunt of industry's "toxic load," is repeated with nearly every mining operation, hydro-electric dam, and clear-cut forest that our voracious economy forces onto the landscape.

The destructive nature and scale of the tar sands operations, and the staggering number of First Nations communities that will be affected by them, make this an industrial project of nightmarish dimensions. The three mines currently operating around Fort McMurray are merely a modest preview of the development yet to come: by 2015, companies are aiming to nearly triple the current rate of production to 3 million barrels a day. By 2030, the goal is 5 million barrels.

The tar sands deposits underlie 149,000 square kilometres of land in three regions: Athabasca, Peace River, and Cold Lake. That's an area larger than the state of Florida; and nearly one third of it, 54,000 square kilometres, has already been leased for development in Alberta. On top of or adjacent to those lands are more than two-dozen First Nations, some already touched by tar sands extraction. Most are covered by Treaty Eight, which was signed in 1899, on the heels of a previous mining frenzy—the gold rush. Treaty Eight affirmed the Métis and First Nations' rights not only to reserve lands and monetary compensation, but also to the continued pursuit of traditional hunting, trapping, and fishing practices. These rights have been steadily eroded by the expansion of the tar sands development.

The erosion of traditional means of self-sufficiency has led some First Nations in the area to seek to benefit from the tar sands development. Fort McKay First Nation, which is located less than fifty-five miles from the three existing mines, has emerged as a willing, if reluctant, participant after years of resistance. The first two mines, owned by Suncor and Syncrude, were established in the 1960s without the consultation or consent of the Fort McKay First Nation. At first, says Chief Jim Boucher, the community fought further development by launching legal challenges in the 1970s that successfully blocked Petro-Canada, Gulf, and Shell from setting up camp in the area. But then, in the 1980s, the fur market that had employed Fort McKay's trappers collapsed, and many became dependent on welfare. Realizing they were already surrounded by mines that would slowly erode the populations of wildlife they hunted for subsistence, community leaders felt they had no choice but to turn to the tar sands.

In 1986, the Fort McKay Band Council formed the Fort McKay Group of Companies, which now pulls in millions of dollars of revenue each year from businesses that service oil companies with everything from heavy equipment to workers' camps. The band council is also in discussion with oil companies about extracting the 600 million barrels of bitumen that lie under their reserve. Fort McKay is rumoured to be the richest First Nation in Canada. "This community's success is completely dependent on oil sands development," says Boucher. "That's the only option."

A similar route has been taken by the band council of the Buffalo River First Nation, located just across the provincial border to the east, where the Cold Lake deposit extends into Saskatchewan. In May of

2007, the council signed an agreement with Access Energy allowing oil exploration on their reserve and traditional use lands in exchange for a position as equal partners in the project and the company's commitment to invest in social infrastructure in the community.

Other First Nations, however, are in active opposition to tar sands development on or near their lands. The Woodland Cree, located near the Peace River deposit in northwestern Alberta, are suing the Alberta government in an attempt to block an eight-fold expansion of Shell's Carmon Creek project. The project's main processing plant is less than ten kilometres from the band's main reserve at Cadotte Lake.

The nearby Lubicon Cree are fighting a Signet Energy and Deep Well Oil & Gas project that would see 350 to 500 oil wells drilled near the 247-square-kilometre parcel of land identified by the provincial and federal governments as future reserve land for the Lubicon.

Regardless of the position they take on specific projects, however, nearly all the First Nations in the area have expressed concern about the pace of development, the lack of consultation, and the regulatory vacuum created by an approvals process that considers every project on a stand-alone basis and never takes into account the cumulative environmental effects of all projects combined.

In February 2008, chiefs representing the nations covered by Treaties Six, Seven, and Eight in Alberta unanimously passed a resolution calling for a moratorium on all new tar sands approvals "until Treaty First Nations have approved a comprehensive watershed management plan and resource development plan for the region."

Beyond the areas where the bitumen will be extracted, tar sands developments will also affect First Nations as far as the Northwest Territories and the BC coast.

More than 1,000 kilometres of pipelines are being planned to supply the energy-intensive tar sands operations with natural gas from the north, and more pipelines are required to bring crude oil from Alberta to refineries and markets in Asia and the United States. The Mackenzie Valley pipeline, a project that has been on the drawing board for decades, is designed to bring natural gas from the Northwest Territories community of Inuvik, on the Beaufort Sea, to Alberta, with the majority of the gas likely to be fed into the tar sands operations. The pipeline will open up the Arctic to natural gas drilling, bringing roads, wells, a transient workforce, and other ecologically and socially disruptive elements to what is now largely undisturbed boreal forest and tundra.

Pipeline ruptures and leaks are a serious concern, as the pipes will be buried under permafrost that is increasingly melting due to climate change. The area affected by the pipeline is home and hunting territory to four First Nations—the Inuvialuit, Gwich'in, Sahtu, and Dehcho—with a combined population of about 15,000 people.

Then there are the dozens of First Nations in British Columbia, none of whom have surrendered their lands through treaties with the Crown, that are likely to become unwilling hosts to Enbridge's Gateway Pipeline, meant to carry oil from Alberta tar sands operations to Kitimat on the west coast for export. If built, the pipeline will cross over 1,000 lakes, streams, and rivers in BC alone and cut across the traditional territory of more than 10,000 indigenous people. Still more First Nations land all along the northern coast of BC would be endangered by oil tanker traffic, which has already increased as natural gas condensate headed east toward the tar sands operations is brought into Kitimat. Critics say that catastrophic oil spills are inevitable should heavy tanker traffic be allowed off the coast.

The race to develop the tar sands is set to dramatically transform the lands of Canada's entire Northwest. Inevitable damage to ecosystems and wildlife will endanger the subsistence hunting and fishing cultures of tens of thousands of indigenous people in Canada. The struggle to stem the growth of tar sands operations—and to develop much higher standards of pollution control for those already in operation—is a project of crucial importance in this country that has sacrificed indigenous people in the name of economic development for too long.

FUCKING IT UP:
THE STATE OF CANADIAN FICTION

Nathan Whitlock
Canadian Notes & Queries

"It is as difficult to foretell the weather in a language as in the skies, and as urgent."
—Cyril Connolly, *Enemies of Promise.*

Writing fiction in Canada, or writing about Canadian fiction, can leave one feeling like the member of some irredeemably marginal group—a model railway club, say, or a choral society. The passion you feel for your own opinions, and your conviction that everyone else in your group is busy *fucking it up*, is sustained in the face of the fact that most people could care less either way. Internal debates—over direction, process, tone, as well as the very makeup and relative inclusiveness of the group itself—are fevered and drawn out, despite the stakes being low enough for a child to step over.

Consider the annual furor sparked by the Giller Prize. Every fall, a few literary pundits turn into the most rabid conspiracy-theorists. (To be fair, I include myself here.) The jury composition is sifted for probable biases, its shortlist analyzed for clues about the direction of the prize. Are they rewarding youth over experience? Experimentation over traditional works? Small presses over big? The instant the victor gets his $40,000 cheque, there is yet more gnashing of teeth over the fact that, yet again, a preening, overrated book prize with tons of establishment money behind it has failed to act as a pure expression of literary excellence. Author-critic Stephen Henighan's assertion, in a notorious column in *Geist* magazine, that "nothing signalled the collapse of the literary organism as vividly as the appearance of this glitzy chancre on the hide of our culture" is typical.

If it notices at all, the outside world treats these tantrums with bemusement or scorn or indifference—more likely, some combination of the three. But what if Henighan is on to something? Being the kind of guy who tends to kneecap his own arguments with self-serving distortions, hyperbole, and fuzzy thinking, it's easy to dismiss him as a crank. But even the looniest Kremlinologist sometimes gets it right. If the complaints of Henighan and others lack perspective, it's just as true that the emergence of the Gillers coincided with a transformation in the way fiction got published in this country—and, by extension, how it got written.

Up to the mid-90s, it was understood that a writer had to get a half-dozen or so books under his belt before he had the readership and craftsmanship to consider himself established. (In a letter written in the mid-60s, Mordecai Richler expresses some embarrassment at the way he was being treated as some august literary figure after a scant three novels.) That idea held until the unprecedented success of a few debut novels, Anne Michaels's *Fugitive Pieces* and Ann-Marie MacDonald's *Fall On Your Knees* among them. Suddenly, fledgling novelists went from being a necessary evil to a potential goldmine. From Roy MacSkimming's *The Perilous Trade: Book Publishing in Canada, 1946-2006:*

> Subsidiary publishers began pursuing the Hollywood blockbuster strategy: out of every ten releases, most will lose money, two or three will break even, and one or two will be highly profitable. If companies spread their nets wide enough, their odds of landing a blockbuster improve. Among movie studios and record labels, this is known as risk reduction.

The late novelist Matt Cohen, while admitting this new situation helped his own career enormously, gave his own take on it in his deathbed memoir *Typing:*

> We live in a period when, for better or worse, most of the realities of writing, publishing, and bookselling are being transformed in order to conform to the demands of money. Editorial lists appear and disappear, books are published in enormous quantities with huge promotional campaigns only to be pulped into oblivion, publishing conglomerates come into existence or suddenly vanish. The reason is always the same: money and profit.

Cohen wrote this nearly ten years ago, but it's difficult to say the situation has changed much over the last eight years, except in one way: profits for Canadian fiction have dwindled considerably, and with them most of those huge promotional campaigns. MacSkimming argues that, for the blockbuster strategy to work, the subsidiary publishers need to have excellent editors scoping out new talent, otherwise they "would still be churning out cookbooks and packaged titles." A quick glance at the newest catalogues from those same subsidiaries shows that, whatever the talents of the editors, "cookbooks and packaged titles" are again the lifeblood of mainstream Canadian publishing.

But this needn't be bad news for the art of fiction, however grim it currently looks for the business of it. Using Harry Lime's notion (famously ad-libbed by Orson Welles in *The Third Man*) that contentment produces nothing better than a cuckoo clock, blockbuster-starved conditions should return critical and creative focus back to the actual writing, where it always belonged. Great art flourishes in lean times, and artists do better in opposition.

But we run into a problem: our culture hates harsh truths. Canadian writers (and readers) prefer to couch their reality in pillowy ambiguities, rocked gently on waves of ambivalence. So while, in theory, the collapse of the blockbuster approach should result in a more hard-fought literature, one less attuned to the needs of international publishers and the whims of Giller juries, such a flowering can only come about if there is wide agreement that the scheme was harmful to begin with. Sadly, there are too few signs of that happening just yet.

Many people still consider the past decade a kind of Golden Age for Canadian fiction. Given the plethora of new voices that gained prominence, there's a shred of truth to that view. Too many of those same authors, however, internalized the idea that to write fiction successfully, one must produce work that appeals broadly and is careful not to stray too far from the most middlebrow aesthetics and politics. As I wrote a couple of years ago on my blog, the kinds of writing that, for the last decade, have been in ascendance in Canada are those that eschew

> all thoughts of genuine transcendence or painful self-awareness for vague dreams of being *slightly better*. Slightly richer (though slightly less concerned with money and material things), living in a slightly more interesting city/country/hemisphere, slightly more knowledgeable about art and history and wine, slightly better-read, slightly more attuned to amusing ironies, and slightly more alarmed by signs of creeping philistinism.

Even some very independent-minded authors felt the pull of this aesthetic. I once heard an otherwise very avant garde author declare that she would not begin writing her first novel until she heard that a particular multinational was interested in publishing it.

And the future? When it comes to something like fiction, it's difficult to predict what is coming in the next decades. Certainly, things are changing, albeit slowly. (I certainly don't think that avant garde writer would say the same thing *now*.) There seems to be a fair amount of awakening and eye-rubbing going on for both writers and readers. There is slightly less hesitation to state publicly that a given literary "masterpiece" is in fact a joyless, derivative slog. After years of getting squeezed out of the biggest retail chains and seeing their star authors poached by deep-pocketed multinationals, smaller presses like House of

Anansi and Coach House are starting to act with a little more swagger. Readers occasionally leave the fat doorstops on the shelf in favour of novels that are livelier, more tightly wound, and that breathe clearer air. The successes of Kenneth J. Harvey's *Inside* and David Bezmozgis's *Natasha* are two excellent examples; neither book was perfect, but with both you had the sense of being immersed in worlds that contained the same stresses and tensions as our own. Younger readers make their reading choices solely according to taste and fashion, with no concessions to the dictates of national culture-building. If they have any loyalties, those are local, generational, and/or aesthetic. The over-the-top success of Rawi Hage is a sign that many readers and critics are remembering what it's like to read fiction that actually *does* something, rather than simply peddle soft ambiguities and inert prose.

But a lot of this is happening in a piecemeal fashion. And there is always the lingering hope that those golden days will soon return, or that, because of the evidence of the odd blockbuster, it's still worth writing for the bleachers. Even some clear-eyed authors and critics continue to wait for entities like the Giller to turn things around, as if they ever could. Certainly, we have become no less resistant to hard truths. One of the biggest books about Canadian writing of the past few years was Noah Richler's *This is My Country, What's Yours?* However well-intentioned, Richler's CanLit travelogue reinforced the notion that all of our celebrated authors are roughly equal in accomplishment and ability, and that *how* one writes is less important than the tradition out of which one works—a comforting idea when expressed on CBC Radio, but one which leaves readers and writers alike to feast on themes.

As for the immediate future, that's a little easier to predict. Given that Anne Michaels, with the astonishing success of her first novel, helped to inadvertently create the situation we've been talking about, it's oddly appropriate that she is, at last, publishing her second, *The Winter Vault*, in the midst of this newly shifting terrain. Here is the publisher's description of the book:

> In 1964, a newly married Canadian couple settle into a houseboat on the Nile just below Abu Simbel. At the time of the building of the Aswam dam, Avery Escher is one of the engineers responsible for the dismantling and reconstruction of a sacred temple, a "machine-worshipper" who is nonetheless sensitive to their destructive power. Jean is a botanist by avocation, passionately interested in everything that grows.
> [. . .]

When a tragic event occurs, nearing the end of Avery's time
in Egypt, he and Jean return to separate lives in Toronto;
Avery to school to study architecture and Jean into the orbit
of Lucjan, a Polish émigré artist whose haunting tales of
occupied Warsaw pull her further from her husband, while
offering her the chance to assume her most essential life.

Now, it's a little unfair to judge a novel on its catalogue copy, so here's
a bit from the book's first page:

The future casts its shadow on the past. In this way, first
gestures contain everything; they are a kind of map. The
first days of military occupation; the conception of a child;
seeds and soil.

Grief is desire in its purest distillation. With the first
grave—the first time a name was sown in the earth—the
invention of memory.

No word forgets this origin.

What all of this suggest is, when it comes to finding our way to a
Canadian fiction that shuns bourgeois piety for more unfashionable or
uncomfortable truths, and that eschews mere phrase-making and empty
exotica in favour of fiction that is sharp and alive and receptive to the
twists and cuts of the modern world, we are not quite out of the woods
yet. In fact, we are still fairly lost.

THE BUSINESS OF SAVING THE EARTH

Chris Wood
The Walrus

When I was a boy, our family owned a summer cottage on Georgian Bay. It was a small, glass-fronted box set on a sweep of grey-pink granite scoured smooth by long-gone ice. Juniper and Scotch pine dug their toes into the rock in front, and behind us a few hardy oaks held arthritic fingers to the wind. It was there that I first heard the dry buzz a massasauga rattlesnake makes when it vibrates the hollow scales at the tip of its tail. My father promptly beat the unfortunate serpent to death with a shovel.

Over the next few seasons, other rattlesnakes met a similar bad end on our property. But then our perceptions began to change. In addition to being endangered, it dawned on us that these elegantly garbed reptiles helped control the mice whose annual winter break-ins left rice-sized black droppings to be swept up each spring from kitchen drawers and cupboard corners. We began, that is, to appreciate the snakes' service as well as their menace (more theoretical than real, in any event). By the end of my youth, any rattler that visited was captured gingerly in a bucket and relocated deeper within the island.

A similar change of outlook is occurring across our entire society. We are rethinking our perceptions of nature, and our place in it. It is dawning on us that we are neither masters of nature nor its victims, but merely another of its artifacts; that its fate is ours. The dark forest of folk tale, the bottomless natural bounty of Canada's founding myths, are being revealed for what they are: a biophysical web as essential to humans as to any other animal. And when we look, we see that this web is rapidly unravelling.

Sometime in mid-September, our species will blast through Earth Overshoot Day, the date when we will have consumed all of the natural goods and services, from fish to trees, that our planet takes twelve months to produce. For the remainder of 2008, we will live off the dwindling stock of earlier years' production. We've been doing this for a larger part of every year since the late 1980s: living on eco-credits, giving scant thought to reducing our ecological spending or paying down our overdraft. Now the bill has come due. Drought ravages a third of the planet; deserts annually devour twice as much farmland as they did thirty years ago. Bio-diversity is fraying, and the fresh water that sustains both it and us can no longer be taken for granted. Our species is hurtling around the sun on a spaceship whose life-support system is grinding toward meltdown. Houston, we have a problem.

111

Are we at least enjoying the ride? As it turns out, not so much. During the past half-century, rising incomes have brought the rich world no measurably greater joy in life. For some groups, notably women, the sense of well-being has actually waned. As wealthy as we may be in North America, people in Nigeria and El Salvador report greater contentment. To the amusement, no doubt, of long-departed sages, we are discovering yet again that man does not live by iPod alone, that no amount of stuff can fill that gnawing hole in the soul where happiness might take root.

This is causing even some of the hardest heads among us to question whether the metrics on which we have gauged our communal and corporate progress for more than fifty years now, those abstractions variously labelled as the gross domestic product and the bottom line, are leading us toward paradise or perdition. A few visionaries even posit an altogether new measure of how we're doing, one they have the temerity to call an "index of genuine progress." If they are right, almost everything we thought we knew about keeping track of our economy, businesses, politics, and relationship to nature may turn out to have been seriously misguided. The good news is that we may at last be on the right track.

None too soon, a group of dissenters has stood back from balance-sheet fundamentalism and adopted a new approach. They call it "ecological economics," a phrase acknowledging that in terms of social, economic, biological, and environmental matters, we really are all in this together. Canada has been slower to act on this insight than some other countries. But even here the facts are becoming undeniable. Despite our vast landscape, it's clear we have few fresh fields to plow or lakes to pump. Especially in our most populous regions, we must now learn to work with what we have—perhaps with less.

Plainly we have been counting the wrong things and putting our efforts in the wrong places. What, then, if we counted things differently? To see where that might lead, I travelled first to one of the most remote and superficially backward places on the continent: the Sierra Gorda in central Mexico.

GOING LONG IN GOOD WORKS

You could fly from Mexico City to the heart of the Sierra Gorda in forty-five minutes, if only you could land a plane anywhere in its 3,800 square kilometres of buckled mountain ridges and plunging ravines. Instead, it's a four-hour bus ride from the nearest city, Querétaro, over a blacktop that climbs through corkscrew turns and hangs over vertiginous scenery until it drops into Jalpan, the Spanish mission town at the heart of the reserve. Near the highest summits are stands of Douglas fir and aspen; along the sierra's eastern flank, jaguar and puma prowl one of Mexico's last old-growth stands. Scores of other endangered species, from salamanders to dazzling macaws, find refuge in cloud-forest waterfalls and the many species of oak in its drier western cascades. Mexico designated this magical region a national protected area a decade ago, and the United Nations conferred world biosphere reserve status on it. But actually preserving the Sierra Gorda's ecology has been much tougher. Some 100,000 people live in the region and own 90 percent of it, most scratching a bare subsistence from its worn-out western slopes. In large measure, it is a private property reserve, a place with special status and international recognition, but one where ground truth is still driven by the prosaic needs and interests of its inhabitants.

Two hours from the highway, over a track that in places fades to bare rock, I meet Doña Juanita. A resilient stump of a matriarch four feet tall in straw hat, grey skirt, and worn black loafers, she shares a small compound of wood and adobe huts with her daughter and granddaughter. Their homes on a windy promontory provide a stunning view into shadowed clefts below. We sit in their open-air kitchen, while the two younger women serve tumblers of cloudy *agua dulce de maguey*. The agave juice ferments into *pulque*, the home-brewed ur-tequila that relieves and perpetuates the poverty of so many households here. Fresh, it tastes like smoky coconut milk. Bowls of peppery, tomato-red broth laced with golden egg yolk strings, and palm-sized tortillas hot from the fire follow. The whole meal, I guessed, grew within thirty metres of this spare home.

For all its beauty, the sierra gives up little to humans without hard effort. Many families keep small herds of thin cattle, whose sharp hooves and voracious appetite for acorns ravage the hillsides. Fields are scratched into slopes as steep as fifty degrees. Burros carry water from a spring at the bottom of the valley up to the family's compound. Doña Juanita's grandson once shared the chores with his sister, but like most working-age males in the region he left to find easier, better-paying work in the city. Other young men slip into America. They may be escaping too soon; life and nature here are showing modest improvements. A new solar panel on the roof keeps the *canciones* coming from a radio, hillsides are being reclaimed by flourishing stands of young pine, and the valley spring has greatly improved. Its flow is clear again, and more reliable.

Martin Granadero, a field manager for one of the NGOs the Mexican government hires to care for the reserve, leads me on a ten-minute hike uphill from the restored spring. In the small valley's upper reaches, hillsides long scored by erosion are now contoured with sinuous terraces, where buffalo grass and pine seedlings take root behind newly planted maguey. "In five years, there won't be any bare ground here at all," Granadero says. "In ten years, it will be another world." Already the stabilized slopes capture far more water for the valley spring and contaminate streams downhill with far less sediment.

The remote valley's recovery owes much to the way Mexico has moved past the notion that ecological and social values are necessarily antagonistic to economic ones, and realized instead the urgent need to get the former onto the books of the latter. In 2003, the government recognized that the Sierra Gorda is one of the irreplaceable "water factories" that supply the country's growing cities and 109 million people. With this in mind, it began distributing $500,000 a year to farmers in upland regions, where rain is captured in streams. Through nonprofit groups like Granadero's employer, Bosque Sustentable, the payments are worth up to $40 a year for every hectare a farmer (or *ejido* collective) agrees to protect from wandering livestock, fire, and foragers. When the program was renewed earlier this year, its goals expanded to restoring biodiversity. Farmers now must also safeguard their woodlots from poachers.

Such eco-payments are increasingly mainstream outside Canada. Costa Rica and Panama also pay landowners to manage their properties for water production. The European Union, New Zealand, and Australia remunerate farmers for a variety of ecological services, including maintaining biodiversity. The United States' Conservation Reserve Program spends $1.8 billion a year, giving farmers an average $50 an acre to restore native vegetation along watercourses, among other activities. Helpfully for trading nations, treaties protect such compensation from sanction in what is called a "green box." Coined by the World Trade Organization, the term has nothing to do with nature, only with permission, as in a traffic light. But the permission is important: because eco-service payments are viewed as legitimate transactions, not baleful subsidies, WTO member countries may introduce them without fear of trade retaliation.

Meanwhile, Bosque Sustentable and its parent, Grupo Ecológico, have discovered markets beyond water for the Sierra Gorda's eco-services. Citing science confirming that young forests capture carbon, Grupo Ecológico has sold carbon offsets to organizations that want to bolster their green bona fides, such as the Triple Bottom Line Investment forum. The money goes directly to the locals who own the forest land. And Grupo has even bigger plans for a "boutique carbon package" with social and environmental elements. Research is under way to quantify precisely how great an improvement in water supply, rare-species habitat, and rural living conditions investors can claim with each unit of the product they buy.

WE ALL LIVE DOWNSTREAM

The exhausted hills of rural Mexico may seem a world apart from rich, prosperous Canada. But look again. Canada's prime agricultural land would fit into an area not much larger than Montana, a state with less than one-thirtieth of our population. Unwitnessed by urbanites, the soils on which Canada's harvests rely are being exhausted five to fifteen times faster than they are being replenished. If our industrial parks generally seem cleaner than their Chinese counterparts, it is mainly because we've been off-loading our most polluting businesses, even our electronic trash, to Asia. If you include the portion of our ecological footprint we export, the average Canadian uses four to five times our per capita share of the earth's natural services. Put another way, it would take four or five planets to give every human our lifestyle of flat-screen TVs, big box stores, and drive-through doughnut shops—more in places like southern Ontario, Montreal Island, and BC's Lower Mainland, where we are most densely packed.

Across North America, the housing boom of the new century has exposed the zero-sum nature of our most critical landscapes. For the majority of us, those aren't the roadless tracts at the top of the Dominion map or the deserts of Nevada. Rather, they're the green spaces that begin just beyond the last model home. And, as with the Sierra Gorda, most of those green spaces belong to someone and are already fully occupied.

Two provinces, Ontario and British Columbia, have wielded their legal fiats to declare no-go zones for development around their biggest cities. The newest, Ontario's 7,300-square-kilometre greenbelt, fish-hooks west from the Niagara River around Toronto and back east as far as Cobourg. Inside it, the wheat and corn fields where I biked as a teenager have mostly disappeared beneath spray-on communities branding themselves as tranquil oases insulated from the noisy complexity of urban living. Beyond the greenbelt, real estate companies have already banked much of the unprotected farmland for future leapfrog development.

Carol Cowan and her husband, Ken Anderson, live just outside the greenbelt in the stone house Carol's great-grandfather bought in 1874. They moved to the 80-hectare farm southwest of Waterloo four years ago when Carol's father turned eighty-seven. Ken commutes to a Toronto law practice; Carol raises calves organically. "We didn't want the farm to go out of the family, and we didn't want it to become part of the housing development going on as a result of the Toyota plant down the road,"

Carol told me last spring. Serene in a blue denim smock under a halo of short white hair, she had just delivered the first of some fifty calves she would midwife over the coming days.

Ontario's greenbelt, like BC's Agricultural Land Reserve, was drawn on the map of the politically possible. Nature's map follows a different terrain. The creek that crosses the pasture behind Carol Cowan's weathered brown barn, like scores of other brooks trickling over southern Ontario's farm country, is the functional equivalent of Mexico's mountain "water factory." It collects nature's supply of rain and snow from the couple of hundred hectares of farmland it drains, and delivers it to the Nith River, a kilometre down the concession road. Along with the waters of other creeks, the Nith flows into the Grand River. More than 800,000 residents in the surrounding four counties rely mainly on the Grand for water; 500,000 more are expected to join them by 2030. The importance of the creek coursing through Cowan's pasture land to their future is no less for its being excluded from the official greenbelt.

Nor does inclusion in the agricultural greenbelt keep the capillaries of Ontario's water factory from becoming clogged. When cattle gather at a creek to drink, they churn the banks to mud. Fields worked to the water's edge afford no shade for cool-water-loving native fish. Rain that falls on soils laced with fertilizers or pesticides becomes infused with them from furrow to stream. All three factors contribute to the dead zones that have returned to Lake Erie, to which the Grand River contributes a quarter of Canada's share.

Ontario's Grand River Conservation Authority enjoys a reputation as a leading model of watershed governance. Like Mexico, it's been taking a little of the money it receives to maintain recreational areas and manage the river, and giving it to farmers to help keep the basin's water capillaries clean. Carol and Ken received about $5,000 to erect fences along their creek to keep cattle a few metres back from the bank. Inside the fences, the authority planted a hundred burr oak, silver maple, and tamarack saplings that are now growing future shade. Despite her pro-conservation leanings, the fourth-generation farmer swallowed hard before agreeing to give up any of her working land to creekside repair. "People whose income comes solely from their farms," Carol says, "[are] going to need to get a lot of money to change."

And more change will be needed. Ontario has already lost many of its water-capturing capillaries. Some eighty species at risk live in the Grand River watershed, along creeks like the one Cowan maintains. But it would take only one farmer upstream or down who doesn't buy into the same standard of stewardship to undo her good work.

I asked the conservation authority's Martin Neumann whether enough of southern Ontario's natural water factories were being preserved to carry its bursting suburbs through the summer droughts that are growing longer and more frequent. "No," he replied. "We'd better crank it up, significantly."

DOZING BY SATELLITE

Flying across the country, the Prairies seem comparatively wide-open, virgin territory. But touch down in Winnipeg and drive west, and you are soon disabused of this impression. Here, too, almost every inch of the Prairie Pothole Region is spoken for. The shallow marshes and vernal pools that give the area its name shelter the deer, waterfowl, and less-charismatic creatures whose variety is the definition of biodiversity. And like riverbanks farther east, they protect watercourses and communities downstream from the leakage of industrial agriculture. The same runoff cocktail depleting oxygen in Lake Erie contributes to soupy blooms of blue-green algae in Lake Winnipeg. But with grain prices up at last, many farmers eye the income locked beneath the few remaining sloughs and fire up the dozers. Potholes are shrinking fast, both in number and size.

"There was more brush broken last winter than I've seen in many years," Cam Henry told me one spring morning as we sat in his tidy farm office, forty-five minutes northwest of Brandon, Manitoba. Henry's granddaughters, aged two and three, could one day be the fifth generation of the family to work the land. This operation is on another scale than Cowan's: about 1,700 cultivated hectares produce seed barley, wheat, canola, and flax. After breaking and draining most of the farm's potholes over the years, the Henrys have left 200 or so hectares of slough, creek bottom, and woodlots untouched—for now. But piles of new slash down the road are a ready reminder that their neighbours continue to drain the prairie.

There's an understandable eagerness to take advantage of the return of good grain prices, but that's not the only change threatening the potholes that remain. There's technology, too. "Automated steering," Henry tells me. "It's run off satellite, and it's driving machinery for us. You go to the end of the field, you turn it on, it goes to the other end of the field; it'll turn itself around and come back. But it wants to run in straight lines. Every time you come to an obstacle, you have to turn it off. You can't drive around a slough. So there is a suasion to take those things out."

Helping Henry and some others resist that "suasion" as prices rose over the past three years was Alternative Land Use Services (ALUS), a one-time test program funded by the provincial and federal governments that paid farmers by the acre to drive around sensitive wetlands, keep cattle and machinery out of creeks, plant cover on steeper slopes, and leave patches of native prairie unbroken.

The money was a fraction of what some of the land might have earned in crops. Indeed, with tillable acres earning $100 in profit at harvest time, Henry expects "some young guys would still break them [potholes] up at $50" an acre in eco-service fees. "It'd be 'I don't want to drive around it.'" Still, he contends that the payments tip the balance for many farmers like himself, who are predisposed to give a little ground to nature. But now that ALUS is gone, his family might take a second look at the cost of leaving 200 hectares unbroken. His question for urban Manitobans downstream: "Should we do this alone? Or are you going to help me out with it?"

THE PARASITE'S DILEMMA

Bill Rees, the University of British Columbia biologist who invented the idea of an ecological footprint, has an uncomfortable analogy for the fix we're in: he calls it the parasite-host relationship. "The economy," he explains, "has become parasitic on nature." The problem for the parasite, of course, is that it can't become so successful that it kills off its host. Then it perishes, too. Humans, he fears, may be too successful to be good parasites.

Clearly we have to stop destroying our host; saving as many of Earth's functioning biological factories as possible is a good place to start. If cities need some of the private landscapes around them put into eco-services instead of potatoes, however, they will need to secure the cooperation of the owners and occupiers. "We prefer the system where I agree to provide you something for a period of time and you pay me for it," says Cam Henry, likely speaking for many farmers. Indeed, paying farmers and others to cultivate nature is one way to give our host a shot at living.

But devils lurk in the details of buying and selling Nature Inc.'s product line. Ecosystems are never simple to start with. Casual observation reveals that tree-shaded, grass-banked brooks flow cooler and cleaner than streams exposed to the sun and trampled by hooves. But scientists have trouble putting a reliable number to the degree of difference a particular change in landscaping or vegetation will make to water downstream. I found nearly identical experiments under way in Manitoba and Mexico to answer that exact question.

The greater problem of low confidence in the unproven currency of any new eco-service has triggered successive crises in the world's biggest eco-market: the $60-billion Kyoto-mandated global trade in carbon credits. Enthusiasm for carbon trading has spawned its own ecosystem of carbon practices among financial houses. They trade in credits supposedly underwritten by tonnes of carbon removed from, or not released into, the atmosphere. Backing some are technology investments such as the proposed new carbon scrubbers. Others rest on eco-services, the capture and sequestration of carbon in forests or agricultural cover.

Vancouver consultant Aldyen Donnelly helped broker North America's first credit sales for cropland (in Iowa), and for carbon captured at a natural gas power plant and pumped underground (in Texas). But the way the carbon marketplace emerged has left her disenchanted. Governments gave away too many credits to begin with. Vendors too often sold the carbon equivalent of the Brooklyn Bridge. At best, they were what Donnelly calls "anyway tonnes," carbon that would have become trees or switchgrass without any encouragement at all. "I believe we're pursuing the wrong model," she says now.

Donnelly has an intriguing alternative: ecological product standards similar to consumer protection laws that eliminated lead in gasoline, or limit how much water can be injected into processed chicken (you didn't know?). This version would require businesses to meet or beat a target score on their product lines' ecological footprints. Potentially modelled on the multi-scale LEED score that rates new buildings according to environmental benchmarks, her eco-standard would ask industries to account for half a dozen key impacts, including carbon balance, water consumption, and effect on biodiversity. When it's applied to a handful of big-footprint industries (cement, transportation, energy, and food all make the list), Donnelly says, "You capture about 95 percent of the problem." Already Britain's Tesco food chain has taken a step in this direction, promising to reveal to customers the lifetime carbon "content" in each of its tens of thousands of products.

A more prosaic way to compensate landowners for saving critical bits of ecosystem has been around for decades. When CBC cameraman Stephen Digby retired, he began to consider the future of an 80-hectare woodlot he and his wife own near Lake Simcoe in south-central Ontario. The property is unprepossessing. Malnourished second-growth balsam and juniper spread their roots over exposed limestone plates webbed in mossy duff. To a biologist, however, it's a prime specimen of a shrinking type of rare alvar ecosystem. Digby expected some future owner would "log it off for everything that was there, and what was left would be taken over by the limestone industry." Instead, any potential future owner will find that "everything that could be protected above the surface, under the surface, and at the surface," as Digby puts it, belongs to the Nature Conservancy of Canada for the next 997 years. The Digbys kept the title to their property and received a tax receipt for $25,000. That's it. Similar easements have brought an area the size of Lake Ontario under the protection of the Nature Conservancy, Ducks Unlimited, and other conservation trusts.

Other tax levers could do much more to influence greener choices. The National Round Table on the Environment and the Economy advocates a general shift in taxation away from income onto activities with a heavy ecological footprint. The federal Liberals' proposed carbon tax would do this, but there are countless other ways to apply the idea. Why, for example, should only farmers be rewarded for giving up space to nature? Backyards are green space, too, as are wildlife migration corridors—now being lost—in urbanizing regions. Why not give a tax break to the corporate campus turned over to wild bird meadow instead of lawns?

SALAMANDERS BY THE ACRE

One way to answer the hard question of how much a particular patch of ecosystem is worth is to go out and try to build one just like it. That's Wildlands Inc.'s game. The California-based company sells eco-credits based on a portfolio of ecosystems its 100 employees have banked from Georgia to Washington state. It earns profits on 30,000 acres occupied by such endangered species as Swainson's hawks, kit foxes, and giant garter snakes. "We're a convenience store source," says sales director Jeff Mathews, a cheery guy in khakis and denim shirt. "If you buy a credit from one of our banks, you're buying a commodity."

Ninety minutes south of Vancouver, the I-5 traffic whines unceasingly along the base of a kilometre-and-a-half-long arrowhead of green land, where a river divides in its last rush to the sea. The former marsh was drained a century ago, and this bit was farmed until this year. Most of the rest is now the Port of Everett, commercial farmland, and a resting place for the skeletons of old construction equipment. Among the lost eco-services has been a critical layover moment in the life of chinook salmon, when young fish leaving their natal freshwater streams linger in tide-washed marshes to allow their gills to adjust to the saltier sea.

This spring, as collapsing salmon stocks prompted the US to declare an unprecedented fishing ban along its west coast, Wildlands set about turning this particular farm back into salt marsh. When the transformation is complete, the company plans to sell the restored chinook habitat in the form of offset credits akin to those proposed by Grupo Ecológico.

The $3-billion market for the company's services exists because US laws allow developers in certain cases to destroy wetlands or rare-species habitat if they create functioning substitute habitat elsewhere. Offsets are typically certified in the same or a similar ecosystem at a ratio above one to one. California kit fox habitat in Wildlands' catalogue carries a sticker price of $5,000 to $7,000 an acre; stream habitat for giant garter snakes costs $40,000. Replacing an acre of vernal pool in one of America's fastest-growing counties, near Sacramento, will set you back $300,000 or more.

Robert Costanza would say that all these ideas, from ALUS to Wildlands, are trying to do the same thing: close the accounting gap between the biophysical world and the economic one. Costanza is a fervent ecological economist. He was the first in his profession to rough-guess the global economic value of nature's services, from waste assimilation to water provision to food supply. His sum in 1997 was $33 trillion per year, more than the world's GDP. He believes that relationship hasn't changed—our debt is simply bigger now—and we must account for the Earth's services or lose them.

The solution doesn't lie in land-rush privatization of every lake and stream, Costanza says, but neither is it to be found entirely in government agencies. He advances a third state: "propertization" through new public institutions with property title to our natural and social-capital assets, and a fiduciary duty to preserve these assets and any wild inhabitants. Such "common asset trusts" would charge those who use our shared resources—towns, for instance, that release waste to be assimilated in rivers—and use the money to keep nature functioning. A bill modelled on Costanza's idea (with the additional feature that it would pay citizens an annual dividend for the use of their share of the commons) is before Vermont's General Assembly.

A NEW COMPASS

Compelling all this invention is the fact that economic navigation-as-usual, has failed us so badly—possibly fatally. Some of the most plausible narratives of how mankind will experience the century ahead run through desperate wars over dwindling resources, fought until we have reduced ourselves to numbers the planet can actually sustain. Oceanographer Andrew Weaver has his own analogy for this: he thinks we're like one of those algae blooms in the Gulf of Mexico that gorges on nutrients for hundreds of square kilometres and then collapses. This is where selective accounting has led us.

Businesses, seldom required to account even partly for benefits drawn from intact ecosystems, have little incentive either to restrain their use of them or pass on the cost to customers. As consumers, we see few sticker incentives to choose a product made at sustainable ecological cost over environmental train wrecks. The same is true for other values that make a real difference to life: the opportunity to spend time with our families even as we provide for them; the warmth we feel in greetings from our neighbours; a moment alone in a sunlit glade.

These material omissions partly account for the misdirection we've been getting from the main compass of conventional economics, the GDP. Sensors able to record values the GDP ignores are at the heart of the new models of economic gyroscope. They go by various names— Genuine Progress Index, for example—and all of them owe a large debt to an instrument a feudal monarch decreed should guide his 700,000 subjects in a tiny and frankly dirt-poor mountain kingdom.

I met the Canadian who helped create Bhutan's Gross National Happiness Index in the felicitous surroundings of a faux British pub near his office in Victoria, BC. Michael Pennock is an epidemiologist; he studies populations. Invited to spend three months helping Bhutan's Buddhist officials draw up a survey to determine the kingdom's state of bliss, he found he had to recalibrate how he understood happiness. In Bhutan, he explained, "they say 'well-being' is something you should be able to experience on your deathbed, when your health is totally failing you."

The Bhutanese certainly had material desires (TV and Internet have recently come to the kingdom), but their state of well-being drew from less tangible sources. Good health did make a difference after all. But so did economic security, the reliability of a livelihood more than its extravagance. Work, understood as doing something useful with your time, also made for happiness, although not if occupational obsession stole hours from parenting, community involvement, worship, or spending time in nature. Trustful communities were a less obvious but important factor.

In comparing Bhutan's aspirations to those driving most North Americans, Pennock recalled decades of research in the US and Britain showing that neither society was any happier for the doubling of its

GDP over the past half-century. Casting a wry look over his own history of 60-hour workweeks, he concluded, "There is a lot of good empirical evidence that we have been going down the wrong path."

Happiness may be a fuzzy benchmark for the Western mind, but Canada is about to get its first serious rival to the GDP. With support from the Atkinson Charitable Foundation and the patronage of Roy Romanow, a loose confederation of academics, statisticians, and other specialists has been assembling a Canadian Index of Well-Being. When launched in the spring of 2009, it will attempt to triangulate our progress along no fewer than sixty-four indicators covering values from health and ecological function to civic engagement and community vitality. When we last spoke, Romanow was hoping to reduce those to a single number that would "resonate around the water cooler," and compel a more balanced performance from Canadian leaders. "When you're driven by straight economics," the former Saskatchewan premier said, "you don't take these other things into account. But if there were public acceptance of the Canadian Index of Well-Being—and 'the CIW is up' or the 'CIW is down'—Canadians would want to know why. Political actors will have to tailor their policies to fit that."

"I don't think we'll change our politics before we change our goals," Robert Costanza says. "In pursuing the wrong goals, we are heading over a cliff." But getting ourselves to give up stuff will be a hard sell if we can't be brought to see that most of it has been a disappointment anyway.

MR PRIME MINISTER ...

"I'm a biologist," says Bill Rees. "I don't think we're in any way exempt from the sort of negative feedback loops other species have experienced." He tries to be equally clear-sighted about what, if anything, might persuade us to change course. "The reality is that historically it's tragedy, catastrophe, that really moves people. The only other thing that makes people change behaviour, oddly enough, is price increases." In other words, if we don't wish to snuff out our evolutionary experiment, we must face the true cost of preserving a functioning habitat at the checkout.

Now is the moment to call up a rescue posse unlike any other—to draft our country's brightest ecologists, its experts on social and natural capital, its least dogmatic economists, most inventive financiers, and creative lawyers and direct them to come up with a repair plan. Let them make what inquiries they think necessary, look at what other places have tried, but in the end devise ways for us to begin to do three things: pay in full for the eco-services we receive in every product or service we use, ensure the extra money goes to begin paying off our overdraft at the bank of nature, and permanently repair our economic guidance system. Houston, call in the bean counters!

Correcting a century of accounting error is a large task. Just bringing the services we get from ecosystems onto the books would affect every person in Canada. Some of the issues (putting a "price" on nature) are emotional. The short-term effect will be unpopular: costs will rise. Thus few politicians with ambition would accept such an assignment, and yet no honest appraisal of our situation can come to any other conclusion but that we must try.

Happily, Canada has an institution for tackling this kind of job. The prime minister should promptly call into being a Royal Commission on Sustainable Economics. He should give it no more than five years to design a fair but effective means to put our economy on a pay-as-you-go footing for nature's services, and on track to eliminate our ecological deficit.

The next election may be fought over how to begin settling just part of our eco-tab. The Liberals would tax carbon emissions; the Tories want to cap them and trade reduction credits. This is somewhat like debating which colour to use when replacing a light bulb on Apollo 13. Beyond financial crises, beyond riots for food and the madness of King George, the prospect of losing our life-support system is the one truly existential test our society, arguably our species, will face in this quarter-century. Any prime minister who does not at least prepare to meet it fails his moment in history.

THE SNAKE AND I

We live, most of us, in mythology. In Canada, our myth is that we have few people and lots of geography. Just look at a map, especially all that "empty" room in the North. But our myths are giving way to new facts on the ground.

Jim Webb knows his part of our northern geography particularly well. From his home in BC's Peace River country, it's an eight-hour drive to meet clients in High Level, Alberta. He's married to a Cree woman and has spent three decades consulting with First Nations on how they can secure title to their traditional territories. He's also spent a lot of time studying the map of Alberta, and he's noticed something. What with existing commitments to parks and forestry, expanding resource development, and the pressure to balance that activity by protecting other areas, "Alberta will not be able to set aside sufficiently large areas for conservation and return significant areas of land to First Nations."

With that in mind, Webb's current clients, the Little Red River Cree Nation and the Tallcree First Nation, propose what may be Canada's largest eco-sale to date. They already hold provincial permits to log 15,000 square kilometres of Crown forest and muskeg wetland astride the Peace River, east of High Level. They're asking Alberta to alter those permits: to let them do less logging and instead protect old-growth forests sheltering wood bison and caribou. The bands estimate the change will cost them $2.5 million to $5 million a year in net income. They think managing the land to preserve its biodiversity and other ecological services should be worth roughly the same amount. They suggest that oil companies could underwrite an arm's-length trust fund that would monitor the health of the land and issue cheques to the Cree.

Garry Mann thinks it's a hell of an idea. He oversees environmental compliance for oil and gas middleweight Nexen Inc. The company extracts deep-bed unconventional crude oil and operates a heavy-oil upgrader. Mann agrees that Alberta should sequester more land from development, even that oil companies should pay for it as a cost of doing business. "Sooner or later, our public accounts do need to monetize the value clean air and clean water provide to a society. My hope is that it would happen sooner rather than later."

I now live in Vancouver Island's Cowichan Valley, a place a casual visitor could easily mistake for Eden. Our wooded slopes and emerald fields seem unspoiled. Our communities are comfortable, if not opulent. There is a mild bustle of development, but not the galloping sprawl that has swallowed the Ontario of my childhood. Yet the casual visitor would be wrong. Logged land is being repurposed as acreage lots, forcing wildlife into dwindling refuges. Warmer days have so reduced our major river that some autumns the salmon cannot pass the gravel bar at its mouth. Despite greater integration than elsewhere, the Cowichan Tribes' claim to much of the valley remains unsatisfied. And the rumble of distant food riots and rumours of peak oil echo even here.

We face what every Canadian community does in this century. We understand we have almost reached the hard bottom of our treasure chest of resources. We are recognizing that "growth" alone does not lead to paradise; perhaps the opposite is true. With a little more honesty, we may see in time the wisdom of the Bhutanese, and of the ages. To speak for myself, I am coming to understand that my place in the garden is only as secure as the serpent's.

CONTRIBUTOR BIOGRAPHIES

KAMAL AL-SOLAYLEE is an assistant professor at Ryerson University's School of Journalism. He was the theatre critic for the *Globe and Mail* from 2003 to 2007 and for *Eye Weekly* from 1998 to 2003. He holds a PhD in Victorian Literature from Nottingham University in England and has taught at the theatre programs of both Waterloo and York universities.

KATHERINE ASHENBURG is the prize-winning author of three nonfiction books and hundreds of articles on subjects that range from travel to mourning customs to architecture. Her latest book is *The Dirt on Clean: An Unsanitized History (2007)*. She is a regular contributor to the Sunday Travel section of *The New York Times* and she writes a column on design and architecture for *Toronto Life* magazine.

KRIS DEMEANOR is a songwriter and performer. He has put out five CDs of original music and toured clubs and folk festivals around Canada, Australia, and Europe, both solo and with his Crack Band. He lives in Calgary.

JESSA GAMBLE is an award-winning science journalist. She has written for the likes of Scientific American and Canadian Geographic. The Canadian Science Writers Association honoured her writing with a 2007 Science in Society journalism award. She lives in Yellowknife with her husband and son.

NICHOLAS HUNE-BROWN is a writer, playwright, and musician in Toronto whose work has appeared in *The Walrus, Toronto Life*, the *Toronto Star*, and other publications. His musical comedy, Just East of Broadway, recently won the Patron's Pick award at the Toronto Fringe Festival.

CHRIS KOENTGES is a freelance journalist. His work is published in leading Canadian publications.

ANITA LAHEY's first book of poetry, *Out to Dry in Cape Breton* (2006) was a finalist for the Trillium Book Award for Poetry and the Ottawa Book Award. As a journalist, she has written for *The Walrus, Canadian Geographic, Cottage Life, Chatelaine* ,and many other publications. She is the editor of *Arc Poetry Magazine* and lives in Montreal.

ALISON LEE is the manager of Good For Her, a feminist sex store in Toronto as well as the organizer of the annual Good For Her Feminist Porn Awards. Between this job and previous work as an adult website reviewer, she can safely claim to have viewed more porn than you even knew existed. More of her writing can be found at alisonlee.ca.

NICK MOUNT is an assistant professor of English at the University of Toronto. A regular contributor to *The Walrus* magazine, his recent book *When Canadian Literature Moved to New York* won the 2005 Gabrielle Roy Award for literature.

DENIS SEGUIN is a freelance journalist and filmmaker in Toronto. He has contributed to a wide range of titles in Canada, the UK, and the US. He is the writer and coproducer of the upcoming CBC documentary *How To Start Your Own Country*.

CHRIS TURNER is the author of *The Geography of Hope: A Tour of the World We Need* (2007) and *Planet Simpson: How A Cartoon Masterpiece Documented an Era and Defined a Generation* (2004). His magazine writing has won five National Magazine Awards, including the 2001 President's Medal for General Excellence. His reporting on culture, technology, and sustainability has also appeared in *The Walrus*, *Time Magazine*, *Utne Reader*, *Maisonneuve* and *Adbusters*. He lives in Calgary with his wife, photographer Ashley Bristowe, and their two children.

LORI THERESA WALLER is a writer and researcher living in Ottawa. Her work has appeared in *Peace and Environment News*, *The Dominion*, and *Briarpatch Magazine*. In 2007, she travelled throughout Alberta with the Sierra Youth Coalition to learn about the effects of tar sands developments on communities there.

NATHAN WHITLOCK is the author of *A Week of This: A Novel in Seven Days* (ECW Press). His writing and reviews have appeared in the *Toronto Star*, *Globe and Mail*, *Report on Business*, *Maclean's*, *Maisonneuve*, and elsewhere. He is the Books for Young People editor for *Quill & Quire* magazine and the fiction editor for *Driven* magazine. He lives in Toronto.

CHRIS WOOD has been a professional writer for more than thirty-five years, covering major international and Canadian events as a journalist for *The Walrus*, *Maclean's*, *Reader's Digest*, the CBC and many others, as well as writing more than half a dozen books, ranging from business memoirs to young adult mystery fiction, in addition to his two highly acclaimed nonfiction studies, *Dry Spring: The Coming Water Crisis of North America*, and *Blockbusters and Trade Wars: Popular Culture in a Globalized World* (with Peter S. Grant). He makes his home on Vancouver Island.

PERMISSION ACKNOWLEDGEMENTS

"Too Poor to Send Flowers: The State of Canadian Theatre" originally appeared in *Canadian Notes & Queries* (December/January 2008) copyright © 2008 by Kamal Al-Solaylee. Used with permission of the author.

"The New Death Etiquette" originally appeared in *Toronto Life* (October 2008) copyright © 2008 by Katherine Ashenburg. Used with permission of the author.

"Get a Real Job" originally appeared in *Unlimited* (January 2008) copyright © 2008 by Kris Demeanor. Used with permission of the author.

"Where the Muskox Roam" originally appeared in *Up Here* (December 2008) copyright © 2008 by Jessa Gamble. Used with permission of the author.

"Lost in Translation" originally appeared in *Toronto Life* (August 2008) copyright © 2008 by Nicholas Hune-Brown. Used with permission of the author.

"Helen Koentges" originally appeared in *Swerve* (May 2008) copyright © 2008 by Chris Koentges. Used with permission of the author.

"Last Rights" originally appeared in *Maisonneuve* (Summer 2008) copyright © 2008 by Anita Lahey. Used with permission of the author.

"The New Face of Porn" originally appeared in *This Magazine* (November/December 2008) copyright © 2008 by Alison Lee. Used with permission of the author.

"The Return of Beauty" originally appeared in *Queen's Quarterly* (Summer 2008) copyright © 2008 by Nick Mount. Used with permission of the author.

"The Anti-Socialite: Life with an Asperger's Child" originally appeared in *The Walrus* (September 2008) copyright © 2008 by Denis Seguin. Used with permission of the author.

FURTHER READING

Canadian Business
"This is Not Going to Go Away," Donald J. Johnston, March 17, 2008.
"Crude Awakening," Jeff Sanford, October 27, 2008.

Geez
"I believe in devilled eggs," Angela Long, Issue 10.

Humanist Perspectives
"Punishing Acts of Mercy: Robert Latimer and the Justice System," Gary Bauslaugh, Issue 164.

The Walrus
"Darkness Visible: Ego, ambition, lost souls and nailing the Opposition in Ottawa," Barry Campbell, April 2008. (Other segments of the Barry Campbell memoir *Politics as Usual* appeared in the March and May issues.)

Dooneyscafe.com
"Almost Drowning," Brian Fawcett, March 28, 2008.

The Malahat Review
"Bad Day," Joel Yanofsky, Issue 165, Winter 2008.

Riddle Fence
"God Help Thee: A Manifesto," Joel Thomas Hynes, Issue 2.

Toronto Life
"The Curse of the Aluminum Crystal," Chris Nuttall-Smith, September 2008.
"The Prince of Little Mogadishu," Gerald Hannon, December 2008.

EDITOR BIOGRAPHIES

ALEX BOYD lives in Toronto. He writes poems, fiction, reviews and essays, and has had work published in magazines and newspapers such as *Taddle Creek, Books in Canada,* the *Globe and Mail, Quill & Quire, The Antigonish Review,* and on websites such as *The Danforth Review* and *Nthposition.* He booked and hosted the I.V. lounge reading series in Toronto for five years, and edits the online journal *Northern Poetry Review.* His personal site is alexboyd.com, and his award-winning first book of poems *Making Bones Walk* was published in 2007.

CARMINE STARNINO has published four books of poetry, the most recent of which is *This Way Out* (Gaspereau Press, 2009). His poems have won the F.G. Bressani Literary Prize, the A.M. Klein Prize for Poetry, and the Canadian Authors Association Poetry Award. He the author of *A Lover's Quarrel,* a collection of essays on Canadian poetry, and the editor of *The New Canon: An Anthology of Canadian Poetry.* A new collection of his poetry criticism is forthcoming from Biblioasis in 2011. He lives in Montreal, where he edits *Maisonneuve* magazine